The Christian Executive

By the Same Authors . . .
  The Art of Management for Christian Leaders
  Strategy for Living
  Strategy for Leadership

The Christian Executive

a practical
reference for;

- Christians in
Management Positions
- Leaders of Christian
Organizations
- Christian Educators
- Pastors and Other
Christian Workers

Ted W. Engstrom &
Edward R. Dayton

WORD BOOKS
PUBLISHER
WACO, TEXAS

CONTENTS

of Meetings/Good Communication/The Special Case of Number Two/Should There Be a Number Two?/Some Examples/ The Importance of Number Two/How to be a Good Number Two/How to be a Good Number One/Number Two May Not Become Number One/Who Is Qualified for Number Two?

```
PART III    YOU AND THE ORGANIZATION
```

PART IV   THE LANGUAGE OF MANAGEMENT

Preface

THIS IS THE FOURTH BOOK that we have written together. A great deal of it comes from the day-to-day encounters we have had, not only as executives in a large Christian organization, but also as laymen in our church and teachers in both pastors' seminars and seminaries. Sometimes people ask us where we get the time to write or teach. Our answer is usually something like, "Because we enjoy sharing with others." It is a special blessing and a real privilege to be able to help others along the way.

As was the case in *The Art of Management for Christian Leaders,* this volume is a collection of the *Christian Leadership Letter* which we have edited together for six years. However, in many places we have greatly expanded and rearranged the earlier material.

Our special thanks to Carol Kocherhans and Moye Loya who worked with such consistent skill in preparing the original *Letters,* and to Berva Smith who showed such enthusiasm for producing the manuscript.

Monrovia, California   TED W. ENGSTROM
                                           EDWARD R. DAYTON

Part I

You
and
Yourself

1
Manager
or
Minister?

THIS IS A BOOK addressed to Christian executives—leaders and managers in Christian organizations, be they local churches or other forms of Christian ministry. The leader of every organization is in one sense an executive. *Christian* executives are those who are leading Christian organizations. What is a Christian organization? Our definition is a broad one: a Christian organization is any organization that sees as its *primary purpose* giving glory to God.

Christianity is all about relationships. First, our relationship to our God and Creator. Second, our relationship to one another as members of Christ's body, his church. Third, our relationships to all men. Therefore, one of the first questions every Christian executive must face is, "Am I a manager or a minister?"

The Special Role of the Pastor

As we discuss the question of manager or minister, we first need to recognize the special role of the church and thus, the pastor. Among all organizations in the world, the local church is unique. It accepts as its Christian mandate two apparently contradictory tasks: first, to care for the members of the body of Christ, spiritually, physically, emotionally; second, to send forth these same members to areas of service. The local church which follows Jesus' example of preaching good news to the poor, lifting up the downtrodden, and binding up the wounds of the bleeding will quickly have its hands full just caring for the many people it will attract. When the word gets out about *that* kind of a church, the poor, the downtrodden and the bleeding will come from miles around. The leaders of the local church are continually faced with the unsolvable dilemma of "building up" versus "going forth." Neither can be put aside.

The result of these conflicting roles is a complex organization indeed, and it represents an immensely difficult task for the pastor. The local church has neither the prerogative nor the means of putting the needs of the organization before the needs of the individual, yet at the same time it must not put the needs of the individual before the needs of the organization.

So the answer to our question, "Manager or Minister?" can never be satisfactorily answered for the leader of the local church. He or she is always "manager or minister." The same is not true, however, of other Christian organizations.

The Christian Organization

In many ways the so-called "para-church" organization is a response to the dilemma faced by the local church. To "go forth" on the Lord's business, there needs to be a cadre of men and women who are equipped for the task and motivated toward it. Probably one of the reasons why mission organizations spring up outside the context of denominations is that they can attract to themselves the "healthy" recruits they need.

Whereas the local church must continually struggle to maintain both an orientation to the task and a people orientation, the Christian organization by definition is *primarily* oriented toward the task. This does not mean for a moment that the individuals within that organization do not have a Christian responsibility toward one another. It does mean that the organization is focused first on its purpose.

Start with Management

Minister or manager? Unfortunately, too many Christian organizations are led by men or women who have a gift for ministry and little training (or perhaps even inclination) for management. Witness the large number of leaders of Christian organizations who are ordained. Of course, ordination does not exclude a person from having management gifts and skills, but it does give an indication of the leader's basic training and probable bias. This emphasis on ministry or ministering to people may lead the organization back to the same dilemma that the local church faces.

A Manager As Minister

But assuming we have selected the best *managers* we can find to lead the organization, do we not still have a responsibility to minister to each other? Of course.

Even a tough army top sergeant knows that *people* are the ultimate key to a successful organization. A great deal of thought and study has been given to how to make people more productive by giving them more satisfying work, by providing adequate remuneration, by placing them in an environment which is conducive to their well-being, and by generally helping them to feel good about themselves, the organization, and their task. Most of the management literature indicates that all of this is done for the good of the organization, or the good of the product. This is probably only a half-truth. Most men and women, be they Christian or non-Christian, enjoy helping others and seeing others operating effectively.

But what about the *Christian* manager? If he or she is leading an organization made up of members of the same mystical body of which he or she is a part, is there not some special relationship implied?

What guidelines can we give for this situation?

Guidelines for Ministry

With the exception of the local church, as we discussed above, we must always begin with the organization. After all, the organization and its purpose are intimately and ultimately entwined. If we give up the organization, by definition, we must give up our purpose. Therefore, if the organization is to survive, ultimately the *organization* must have first priority. There will be times when the organization will permit itself to be diverted from its task for the good of the individual. However, if the leadership of the organization believes that what the organization is about is part of God's purpose, eventually the sometimes tragic choice between the good of the organization and the good of one individual must be settled in favor of the organization.

It does not follow that the manager never puts aside purposes for people. *Most* situations which will face the Christian manager will not be a clear-cut question of the choice between the organization and the individual. Usually they will be situations in which he or she can respond to the need of the individual without jeopardizing the organization. But nevertheless, the task is that for which the organization exists.

Where to Begin

But there are a number of things that we can do.

How do we minimize the tension between caring for people and accomplishing our goals?

Start with the selection of staff. Generally, there are one or more of three reasons why an individual seeks to join the Christian organization: first, he may have a strong belief in the organization's purposes. Second, he may be attracted by the idea of working with other Christians in an environment which is usually less competitive and where, by definition, people are more likely to be concerned for the individual as a person. Third, there will be those who come to work in the Christian organization because for one reason or another they could not succeed in a secular organization. Too often, the Christian organization's salary structure is such that it tends to attract people in this last category.

Since this is the case, try to ascertain each candidate's primary reason for joining the organization. Go for excellence! Look for the best people available. Concentrate on those who have a high sense of Christian calling balanced by necessary skills and experience. One is not a replacement for the other. Both are needed.

Demonstrate in your own life style what you expect of others. Model the desired characteristics, your own way of carrying out the business of the organization. The marks of a Christian organization are intangible. A gospel text on the wall doesn't make the organization effectively Christian. Rather it is a spirit that is evident among the people, a spirit that is constantly engendered, prayed for, and modeled by those who are responsible to set the pace.

Whether it be the gentle way in which two secretaries working in a three-person office care for each other's needs or the enthusiasm for getting a good job done, there is something about the truly Christian organization which is shown just in the way people act.

A good example of a place where the leader can be a model is in the dimension of prayer. Many Christian "professionals" come to view prayer within the organization as almost a ritual. Meetings may be opened and closed with prayer, or they may be begun with a corporate devotional time. Such rituals can quickly hide the vast riches of fellowship available. Recognize that the "business" is carried out not only in the presence of the Almighty, but that he is very interested in what is going on. The leader who has the ability to include prayer as a natural part of the organizational life will encourage others to do the same.

In our own organization, each department begins the day with corporate prayer. Once a week all of the headquarters office, over 400 people, meet together for an hour of corporate worship and sharing. A little arithmetic will show what a large investment in salaries that is. It's worth it.

Encourage members of the organization to minister to each other, but let it be in response to felt needs, not pushed. Move into situations carefully and cautiously, guided by the Holy Spirit. Unless you are invited, be careful not to move too quickly into personal situations. For example, don't pry into the family affairs of the staff; enter in only as you may be asked for counsel, guidance, and advice.

We need to be sensitive in this area. Many times people will come to us with a personal problem, but it will be the last thing on their agenda for discussion. When the manager senses a person's need, or that he has more on his mind than he is talking about, it is appropriate to remain silent if the person does not open up.

Recognize that you are an authority figure. We need to remember that although we are Christian brothers and sisters, the manager or leader is a significant person in the life of the staff members. A leader *is* responsible for the person's well-being to the extent of his or her salary and working situation. An authoritative role may be forced upon each manager. Some of your staff will feel more "ministered to" if they see you as a peer. Others will need a father (or mother!) figure. The latter have a need to know that someone is in charge and that their personal welfare is in good hands.

Don't use "Christian" manipulation. Because many staff members come highly motivated to be workers in God's kingdom, we may be tempted to use this motivation inappropriately. Because it is the "Lord's work" does not give us license to demand the individual's personal hours to work consistent unpaid overtime, nor to expect that all our pronouncements should be accepted as divinely inspired.

Finally, be a lover. St. Augustine suggested, "Love God and do as you please." His assumption, of course, was that if we loved the Lord with all our mind and heart and strength that what pleased us would please him. How do we know we love God? By how we treat each other. "A new commandment I give to you, that you love one another. . . . By this all men will know that you are my disciples" (John 13: 34, 35). Jesus said that. We can't improve on it.

For Further Reading

Jim Johnson's *The Nine-to-Five Complex* or *The Christian Organization Man* gives some good insight.

2

You
and
Your Job

BEGINNING A NEW JOB can be a lonely experience. No matter
how cordial your reception or how friendly the negotiations
which led to the job, there is always that area of uncertainty. "Will
I be accepted? Was this really the right move? Is this really the
Lord's leading for my life?"

This is just as true for the pastor going to a new church as it is
for a Christian executive taking up a position in a "parachurch"
organization.

A certain loneliness arises from the feeling that you don't have
control of your job, that you are not really on top of things.

Where to Begin?

How *do* you get control of your job? Where do you begin?
Obviously, the place to "begin" is quite a few months before you
actually start a new job. There were many questions which should
have been asked in trying to understand how you might fit in
God's economy. It is to be hoped you have compared the situation you face with your own experience and skills. You have
listened to the representatives of the organization or church as
to their needs and expectations. You have formed some sort of
a picture of how the world is going to be different because *you*
are going to be working in this job.

But suppose you have done some or all of that, and next week
you are going to take up your official duties. What do you need

to be thinking about? What questions can you be ready to ask of yourself and of others?

How Much Time Do I Have?

This is the key question! It sums up a large number of variables. The organization has expectations about *what* it wants you to do. It is consciously or unconsciously going to be looking for marks of "success." In the midst of this evaluation is always the question, "When?"

The first few months on the job are the "honeymoon period." The parties need time to get used to each other before the real business of living can begin. But once that time is past, expectations rise very rapidly. If you have entered a new job with an expectation of "changing things," you need to take advantage of this honeymoon period, to know how long it's going to be. But *your* expectation of the length of time needs to coincide with the expectation of the people with whom and for whom you are working.

List Expectations

List expectations as best you know them. What were the primary reasons you were invited to take this job? What were the expectations of the people who invited you? What are your goals?

Look out for verbal fog! We Christians can conceal all kinds of expectations with spiritual language that is also vague. Do your best to frame expectations in terms of actions, behaviors, and accomplishments that can be measured. Certainly you want to be a "good pastor" or an "effective leader," but what does this mean? What does a good pastor do? How does an effective executive do his or her job?

List assumptions, too. What were *their* assumptions? Were they expecting you to be a one-person show? Were they assuming that you would be a new broom sweeping away old problems? Or did they perhaps expect you would continue the old order of things? What did the letter of invitation say? Did you have an exchange of correspondence that modified your initial invitation?

What were *your* assumptions when you accepted the job? Were you expecting to follow in the established tradition, or did you see this as an opportunity for the organization to do some new things? Did you see yourself coming in as a leader or a follower?

With these two lists in front of you, your expectations and assumptions, and those of the organization, what are the discrepancies? If you had some high expectations of the organization which you did not feel able to share at the time of your coming, these two lists will be d'ifferent. What steps are needed to make them the same? Again comes the key question: "How much time do I have?"

Start with the Basics

Something *very* basic is a *job description.* If you don't have one, you should![1] If the organization has never used job descriptions, then do the best you can to write your own and review it with those to whom you report. What is the general purpose of your task? What are your specific goals? How much responsibility do you have? What are the supposed qualifications for the job?

If you do not have an *organization chart,* make one (see Chapter 18). Who reports to you? To whom do you report? Such a chart is supposed to show lines of authority and responsibility. Like most simple diagrams, however, there are some pitfalls. The fact that someone "reports" to you, for example, does not necessarily mean he/she will be willing to accept your leadership.

A way of picturing the situation at a deeper level is to ask the question, "Whom do I *relate* to?" Take a blank piece of paper. Draw a circle in the middle. Put your name in that circle. Now draw circles for individuals who are grouped all around you. Draw an arrow *to* them if you need to relate to them and an arrow to your circle if they need to relate to you. Many times both are needed.

Another way to say this is that we need to consider not only the formal organization but the informal as well. There will be key people who can either give you a big lift or put roadblocks in your way. You need to understand who they are and how you relate to them. For example, in a local church situation there will be people who, because of their length of service with the church, or because of previous offices they have held, or just because of their Christian stature, will have a great deal of influence with others. In the nonchurch organization such people

---

[1] For more help on this see our book, *The Art of Management for Christian Leaders* (Waco: Word Books, 1976).

might be certain board members or the leaders of the group. For example, there may be a department head who has no desire to move beyond his/her present position, but has earned the respect of the rest of the organization because of his/her long years of service.

Where Does Success Lie?

Take this same diagram and draw a dotted line to all the people and groups who are dependent on you for their "success." Do the same for yourself; on whom are you dependent for success? Use whatever definition you want to concerning "success." The point is to realize that in order for an organization to operate effectively, there must be people who fit in.

What Tools Do You Need?

Can we remind you again to *pray?* Don't let Christian piety become so routine that you fail to base your *life* on it!

It is to be hoped that you have thought about tools before you started the job. But now that you are working on it, you will no doubt discover many new tools either to help or hinder your progress. By "tools" we don't just mean things like machines, but the norms, procedures, routines that are either implicit or explicit in any organization.

Every organization has its *norms.* By norms, we mean such things as how people dress, how they are brought into the organization, how they are reprimanded, what is expected of them at social functions, how they expect to be greeted. You may not agree with all of the norms of the organization, but it's important that you recognize they exist, and wherever possible, particularly in the early stages, that you attempt to conform to them.

Most organizations have intricate written or unwritten *procedures.* Many times the organization will not be aware that it has such or how complicated they are. These fall into the category of "That's the way we do things around here." One way to discover this is to ask the different people to whom you talk as you go through an orientation time (see below) about the procedures they use. Another way is to ask for a copy of all the written procedures and forms used by the organization. You can then ask people the purpose of the forms and how they work.

The Christian leader works with *people-power, money, experience, information,* and *time.* A shortage or failure in any one of these areas will usually keep you from performing adequately. The most important is *time.* People can be hired, resources can be raised, experience can be developed, information can be gained, but time is not a variable.

What Are the Signs of "Control"?

The first sign of control is a sense that we are *managing our time.* With reference to the job there are three kinds of time: *superior time* (demanded by your leaders); *peer time* (required by those with whom you work); and *discretionary time* (that which is left in your direct control). When you sense a balance between these, this is the first sign that you are beginning to get control (more on this in Chapter 6).

The second sign of getting control is a feeling that you have *adequate information* to carry out your task. Note that we say *adequate.* You will never have enough information. But somewhere along in the process you should make some projections as to the kind of information you will need and set some goals for obtaining it.

The third sign of control will be your sense that you have enough *experience* to carry out your task. Again, you'll never have *enough* experience. But there comes a time when we begin to believe we now have been through enough of the routines and processes to manage the job.

The fourth sign of control is a feeling that you have enough *resources* to carry out your job. This goes along with the fifth sign of control, that you have enough *people-power.* Although in many ways these last two are the easiest things to acquire, if they do not exist in the organization, you will never be able to carry out your job effectively.

Look at Your Goals

These are just *signs.* The real evidence is that you are achieving *goals.* Of course, this assumes several things: that in the very beginning of the job you staked out some goals for yourself and for the organization; that you made them known to the degree they needed to be advertised; and that some of these goals are now *past events*—they have been accomplished; you are moving on to new things.[2]

You Are in a Process

If it has not been suggested to you, try to work out an *orientation schedule* with your superior(s) for the first month of your new job. To whom should you talk? Whom should you interview? What historical information do you have to review?

At the end of this first month sit down and write some goals for the next three, six, and twelve-month periods. These should be goals for yourself, for the part of the organization which you control, and for the total organization. Use these goals to review with your superiors, peers, and subordinates what you believe needs to be done. Have them tell you what they believe needs to be done.

One very good matter that you could raise when talking to old-timers in the organization is, "What questions should I have asked you that I haven't asked?" Many times this will elicit all kinds of information unavailable in other ways.

In all of this make sure that you keep *communicating* upward, sideward, and downward. One of the most overlooked causes of failure is that people don't tell one another where they are and where they hope to go. This is particularly true in the Christian organization, which often has many aspects of volunteerism about it and in which many times the anticipations of the members can be greatly different than the expectations of the leadership. Too often we assume that because we are all part of the same Christian cause, we must all agree on the details as well as the general purpose. The only way to discover whether this is so is to spell out clearly what we are doing and to discover accurately what others are doing.

For Further Reading

It may not seem like a very Christian title, but Philip B. Crosby's *The Art of Getting Your Own Sweet Way* can be a great help. The one chapter on situation analysis is worth the price of the book.

---

[2] If you need more help in personal goal setting, we have discussed this in our book, *Strategy for Living* (Glendale: Regal, 1976).

3 | You and Your Day

IT'S EVERYBODY'S PROBLEM, isn't it? For some people it is a question of "How am I ever going to get all of this done?" For another person it is wondering how he/she will handle the constant interruptions. For a smaller number it is a question of just not enjoying the work that is in front of them. In other words, what we're discussing here is just a continuation of what we covered in the previous chapter.

The feeling is shared by people on all levels in the organization. The junior secretary feels it as she tries to sort the mail, type the letters, file the correspondence, answer the phone, and remember what it is she was supposed to do after lunch.

The middle manager feels it as he/she moves from one apparent emergency after another, gets an important call from the boss, glances at the stack of unread correspondence, and quickly thumbs through it to see if there is anything needing immediate attention.

The senior executive feels it as he/she moves through an endless series of meetings, wonders how to find time to design a new training program, desperately asks himself/herself if there is ever going to be time to please all of the constituency that seems to have a never-ending series of questions and problems.

We Need Some Training

Yes, we do. Some people seem to have been born with organized minds and easy ability to turn off one problem and switch on to another. But most of us need training. If you haven't considered giving such training to all of your staff who are involved in non-repetitive work, then perhaps this chapter will help.

What Are You Supposed to Do?

We need to ask the same questions as when we first moved into this position: what is my job? Make a list of all the things you are supposed to do. If you have a job description, pull that out and see what it has to say. Don't list just tasks. List specific goals with measurable and accomplishable dimensions, goals that have a date when they are going to be done.

Remember it is not how much you do that is important, but how much you get *done*.

Show this list to your boss or your board. Is this what he or she expects you to accomplish? It may surprise you to learn that you have listed some things you are supposed to do that your boss never contemplated. (On the other hand there may be many things you didn't know were your job, that really *are* expected of you.)

What are you *not* supposed to do? You might gather some of this information from the conversation with your boss. It is surprising how quickly we can add all kinds of things to a job. One day someone asks a clerk to do some extra filing, and suddenly, that becomes part of the work. An executive writes a particularly good report and is asked to do it on a weekly basis. Additional duties like these can really detract from your basic goal. There is nothing inherently wrong with them—it is just that they are getting in the way of doing what you are supposed to do.

It's All Right Not to Finish

Over one of the desks in our office there is a sign that says, "A Clean Desk Is the Sign of a Disturbed Mind." Obviously this person doesn't have the "Clean Desk Syndrome"! The point is you don't have to finish everything every day. It is interesting how people differ in this respect. Some people worry if there is nothing left to do at the end of the day. They wonder if they are going to have a job the next day. Other people feel like they are real failures if they haven't accomplished everything. They go home worrying about the next day's work. Find out what your style is and plan your work accordingly. But remember if we are part of an organization that is doing an effective and God-honoring task, there will probably always be more work to do.

Divide and Conquer

Now that you have a list of the different kinds of things you are supposed to do and the goals you are trying to accomplish, divide the list up into things that must be done every day, things that must be done every other day or so, things that must be done once a week, and things that must be done less often. Make a rough estimate for each of these as to how long it is going to take so you will know when to begin each and when you may complete it. These estimates can be refined as you begin to compare how long it actually took you to do the job versus what you estimated it would take. As you go along, you'll get better and better at estimating, which is one of the keys to effective performance.

It might also be a good idea to prioritize these different kinds of tasks. Which ones are *very* important, of high value? Assign these an "A." Which are somewhat important, of medium value? Assign these a "B." That means that all the rest are not so important, of low value. Give them a "C." Share your priorities with your boss to make sure you have some agreement there.

Design a Standard Day or Week

A "standard day" or "standard week" is a prescribed block of time either every day or at certain times during the week when you are going to do certain kinds of work. For example, for an executive there might be a standard day which begins with a fifteen-minute discussion with his secretary, an hour and fifteen minutes to answer the mail without any telephone interruptions, thirty minutes to handle the telephone calls that have come in during the interim, an hour and a half for meetings that the executive requested.

The afternoon might be left free for meetings called by other people or for projects.

A standard day for a pastor might begin as it did with the executive but then move to spending two uninterrupted hours on sermon preparation, followed by an hour of phone calls and correspondence, with some personal "free" time available in the afternoon to compensate for the "normal" meetings of the evening.

The standard day for a secretary might include a fifteen-minute talk with her boss in the morning, fifteen minutes to get the day organized with a Things-to-Do list (see below), an hour and a half of transcribing dictation, one half hour to open, read, and sort the mail, a half hour to get out urgent letters. The afternoon might be set aside for half an hour of filing, half an hour of reading, and two hours for "project work," such as a big typing job or organizing a special program for the executive or pastor.

Most organizations have certain kinds of weekly meetings. Standard days will have to be modified on these particular days.

Now very few standard days will ever turn out to be "standard." But by scheduling certain types of work at certain times we not only know when to begin, but we don't have to feel guilty about stopping. Thus, if a secretary and her boss have agreed that she is going to spend two hours a day transcribing dictation, she doesn't have to feel guilty when she goes home with an hour's worth of dictation still left to be transcribed. She may want to inform her boss the next day that she is behind, but that was in the design of the standard day.

In other words, a standard day is something we depart from, but it also gives us a design that we can fall back upon when we have that terrible feeling of wondering what to do next.

The Things-to-Do List

There is probably no more powerful organizer and tension reliever than the Things-to-Do list. If you spend the first ten to fifteen minutes of each day (or it could be fifteen minutes in the evening) writing down all the things to be done the next day, this immediately gets rid of the question, "What do I have to do next?" Some people like to prioritize such a list using the ABC technique we have mentioned above and to start with the most important things first. Other people use it to fit things into their standard day.

How about a Daily Planner?

If you really want to get organized, think about some kind of a daily planning sheet that not only lists all of your appointments, but puts down things-to-do under categories such as mail, telephone calls (with numbers), things to plan, things to acquire, and so on. You can buy some of these sheets at stationery stores or design your own.

Plan for Interruptions

How, you may ask, can you plan for an interruption? Isn't an interruption, by definition, something that you did not expect? Yes it is, but interruptions are like the weather. You may not be able to predict when they're going to come, but there's a pretty good chance one day it will rain. Which means that your standard day better have some slack in it. Don't plan to do one hour's work in one hour. Or, if you are in the midst of an emergency, and you have only one hour to finish one hour's work, make sure you aren't interrupted. But by leaving some slack and planning for interruptions, you can be a much more gracious person, and the day will go a lot better.

Plan for the Gaps

Every so often we get the reverse of an interruption. We suddenly "run out of work." We haven't really, of course. What has really happened is that we have not planned far enough ahead with things that we are going to do in just this kind of a situation. If you know, for instance, that it is worth your while to do filing when you have at least twenty minutes to do it, then use filing for the gaps. If there is reading that you need to do some time but it's not immediately important, keep it handy in a reading file near your desk. Some people make a practice of reading a number of different books at the same time and keeping them in different places so that they are handy when they have a few free minutes.

How about a prayer list? Maybe the Lord gave you that gap so that you could get on with addressing him specifically about some of the needs you have, the needs others have, or just praising him.

What about Multiple Bosses?

This is a difficult situation to handle, and unfortunately it is usually the junior people who get saddled with it, typically the secretary. If you get work from a number of different people, or are one of those who give work to a person with more than one boss, then it is important that you have a "contract" with each one. In other words, you have an understanding as to how much has to be done, and when you are "contracting" to get it done;

you have set a date when you have promised it. You may not be able to meet it. You may have to change the date. But at least you have an understanding to begin with. Experience will help you to become a better estimator. This means you'd better keep track of your own estimates so that you can become more skilled at this. It is a great feeling to have confidence in your ability to know how long it will take to get a particular kind of job done.

A Work Log Helps

If you have a diverse work schedule, particularly if you are getting work from different quarters, keeping a work log is very useful. It does not have to be complicated. Note the name of the item, the person who requested it, when you received it, when you promised it, when you began work on it, and when you completed it. This will not only be helpful in keeping track of things for you, but it's a great asset if you're ill one day and don't appear in the office—and other people are trying to find out what's going on.

It Takes Experience

But the way you get experience is to decide how to do it better and begin. Now.

For Further Reading

Ed Dayton's book, *Tools for Time Management,* includes a large number of suggestions on how you can be more effective in managing your time, which, after all, is what "getting through the day" is all about.

4

You and
Your
Education

DO YOU HAVE AN EDUCATION? Notice that we didn't ask have you *had* an education, but rather, do you *have* one? Education is the process we all go through to cope with the world in which we live, to enable us to accomplish those things in life that we believe we are led to do.

In this sense we all need a continuing education. Without it we become obsolete. In his *Age of Discontinuity,*[1] Peter Drucker observes that anyone who graduates from college during the '70s will have to retrain at least twice during his lifetime. Drucker is talking about a new group of people whom he calls "knowledge workers." Unlike people whose livelihood deals with skills which may or may not be used the rest of their lives, the knowledge worker is continually faced with refurbishing not only the data that he/she has but his/her ability to work with it.

Drucker further observes that the basic thing the knowledge worker must learn is *how to learn.* The nature of our North American educational system is such that a small percentage of college graduates will continue to learn after they have graduated from college, without any prompting. Unfortunately, the majority of us consider our educations "complete" once we get our degree.

---

[1] Peter Drucker, *Age of Discontinuity* (New York: Harper & Row, 1969).

33

The Christian has a special advantage here. He believes that God is at work in him continually to make him more than he is. ("God is at work—keeps on working—in you, both to will and to work for his good pleasure"—Phil. 2: 13). We are *becoming* people!

Changing Roles

We are all familiar with the tremendous advances being made in the area of technology. Most of us can quote statistics to show that almost 90 percent of the drugs we use have been developed during the last ten years; that the sum of the world's knowledge is continuing to double at a rapid rate, and so on. What is not so obvious is that the number and types of roles we play are also being affected by technological change. Consider the variety of roles expected of the pastor in the local church. He is supposed to be preacher, manager, executor, leader, counselor, exhorter, teacher, planner, laborer, and on it goes.

If you are not presently personally involved in a program of continuing education, now is the time to take action. The longer you wait the more difficult it will be.

Most of us would never consider that our *Christian* education is complete. Don't make the mistake of believing the rest of education is ever complete either.

Education for What?

We can divide education into three basic areas: the task we perform, the system of which we are a part, and the society within which we live.

Education for the task of most Christian executives is primarily concentrated in the knowledge area. In Chapter 19 we will discuss the importance of being aware that leaders of an organization need to grow with the organization. Organizational growth results in a complexity which multiplies many times faster than the actual size of the organization. As we move ahead in our God-given profession, we need to learn more and more about how an effective organization works and all the factors associated with it. We also need interpersonal skills as well as a growing number of basic skills on how to cope with the technology within which we are forced to work, a technology of long-distance phone calls, jet-age travel, new credit systems, and so forth.

What do we mean by *education for "the system"?* Organizations of any size tend to be complex. They have not only internal complexity, but the complexity of their relationships to all of the other organizations to whom they relate. For example, a foreign mission society has home office personnel, home country area personnel, overseas personnel, and a wide variety of relationships to both the home and the overseas church. All these relationships fit together to make up the "system" which is the organization. To survive, this organization must continually adapt itself to changing circumstances. This means new rules, new regulations, new policies, new ways of doing things. It is easy for the Christian leader to miss the changes taking place in the system. We need to stay educated.

We don't often think about *education for society.* But each of us somehow fits into the society in which he/she lives. We have responsibilities toward the society, and the society in turn interacts with us. Any missionary who has spent four years in another country and then returned to his/her home country has experienced "reverse cross-cultural shock." What a difficult process this adapting can be! If we are to be *becoming* people, we have to "be" in a society that is around us. If our Christian response to the world is going to be appropriate to the need of the world, we must understand the society in which we live. To limit our reading and our education to "Christian" books, periodicals, and educational courses will tend to isolate us from the world to which we say we are called.

Who Is Responsible for Your Education?

Most organizations recognize the need to train their new members. Such training will vary from a half-day orientation to an extensive and ongoing program of continuing education. Secular organizations have done far more than Christian ones. At their Tri-City facility in New York, IBM will sponsor and provide a teacher for *any* subject that six of its employees want to learn. IBM has discovered that the very business of being involved in education raises the overall competency of its staff.

Most Christian organizations find it hard to believe that they could afford the "luxury" of such a program. How *does* one assess the need and the value for continuing education programs sponsored by the organization?

Where to Start in the Organization

Start with your purposes and goals! What is your "business"? If you really don't know where you want to go, it won't make much difference how well-trained your companions are.

An organization's purposes and goals should be reflected in job descriptions of some type (there is that need for job descriptions again!). However, recognize that job descriptions are never static. They will be somewhat out of date the day they are written. However, they are a good point of reference from which to analyze where people *are* in terms of where they *should be*.

Of course, there are two ways to fill a job: either find someone inside or outside the organization who already meets the requirements, or train someone to fit the job. One of the major weaknesses of most volunteer organizations is that they fail to invest in training.[2]

What Are the Means of Continuing Education?

Once one decides what the educational need is, the next step is to select from the various means available for training and continuing education. There will be a compromise between what is optimum and what you can afford.

Professional journals and publications are basic to any knowledge worker, secular or Christian. Be selective. Mix in some of the newsletters that attempt to condense and survey in a particular area.

Books in the field are also a must. Some organizations attempt to keep a small organizational library which they rotate among their staff. Supplement this with a book allowance. Anything that can be done to encourage reading on the part of your staff is to be commended. Many churches recognize the need to give a pastor a book allowance. Can Christian organizations who expect their leadership to stay current with the world scene do less?

Information sources selected by someone who is surveying literature in the field and passing on pertinent information to selected staff members are very helpful. Some pastors have members of their congregation underline or clip articles and pass such along to them. The executive in a small organization may

---

[2] We touch briefly on this in our book *The Art of Management for Christian Leaders*.

want to give this task to his or her secretary. The larger organization may even find it useful to have someone specifically assigned to this task.

A wide variety of *professional seminars* is available, from one day to three weeks or longer. Many of these are offered in conjunction with university programs. Get in touch with the continuing education program of your nearby university or ask to be put on the mailing list of universities that offer such programs.

Everyone is familiar with the *sabbatical leave* of the university and graduate school. The obvious fact that the same need exists for *any* knowledge worker has not yet been widely recognized. Perhaps you need to consider such study leaves. Such temporary recesses could be for as short a time as six weeks or a school quarter (ten weeks).

After-hours formal education paid for by the organization is another option. The availability of nearby colleges and universities will, of course, be a consideration. Many cities have state colleges or junior colleges whose nighttime enrollment far exceeds their daytime enrollment.

In-house training programs may be used to teach more specific skills as well as philosophical concepts. There are many sources available on almost any subject. See the yellow pages of the telephone book in the largest nearby city.

Visits to other organizations are extremely useful. Choose organizations in the same field or preferably the ones that are slightly larger than your own and those who are ministering to similar constituencies. Go with a list of questions about the problems you face and be prepared to discuss your own operations with others. Taking a field trip to visit a number of organizations at the same time can be a very rewarding and highly educational experience.

When Should the Organization Pay for Training?

The answer is: when it is requiring a staff member to perform a task for which he or she is not already adequately trained—from learning to operate a new machine to learning how to get along in a cross-cultural experience.

When it is necessary for the staff member to keep abreast of a given field in order to do his/her job. This is where seminars and field trips are useful.

When you believe that it will enhance the total person on his/her job. This is a particularly difficult decision for the Christian organization. For certainly we should be concerned for the whole person. "How?" is not an easy question to answer. When should you pay for additional courses in Bible or theology? The rule here is to try to make people as "whole" as possible.

What about Your Personal Program?

And what about *you?* If you have been away from any formal training program for ten years or more, you may think that it's "too late," but contrary to most of our expectations, one *can* teach old dogs new tricks, particularly if they have once *learned how to learn.* Think about the three areas we mentioned above: education for the task, the system, and society. Where do you stand in relationship to these three? What do you believe God would want you to be doing five years from now? If you haven't gone through this process, this is an excellent time to begin. Going back to school can be a frightening experience, but most men and women in middle-life find it exhilarating once they have begun.

What is it that you are going to have to learn in terms of skill or knowledge ten years from now? How would you go about learning this? Set some personal goals.[3]

How can you integrate the gaining of new knowledge for your job with the gaining of new knowledge for working in society? How many evenings or weekends a month can you set aside for formal training? Would you be better off to put yourself into an extensive one-to-three-week learning experience once a year or to be enrolled in night classes?

CONTINUING EDUCATION CHECKLIST

For the Organization	Yes	No
We have an orientation program for each employee.	—	—
We have descriptions of each job.	—	—
We have analyzed how long it takes to learn each job.	—	—
We have specific training programs to bring new employees up to job level.	—	—
Each executive has a continuing education program and reports progress against it each quarter.	—	—
We purchase books that our staff need for their position-oriented education.	—	—

---

[3] Again we direct you to our book *Strategy for Living,* for help in this area.

	Yes	No
We ask each executive to attend at least one two-to-three-day training seminar each year.	—	—
We have someone specifically responsible for training program management.	—	—

For the Individual	*Yes*	*No*
I have a set of continuing education goals.	—	—
I set aside time to read at least fifteen books in my field each year.	—	—
I subscribe to three or more journals or magazines in my field.	—	—
I have completed one college-level course during the last twelve months.	—	—
I have thought about and done some planning for the task I will have ten years from now.	—	—
I keep a selected reading file with me on trips away from the office.	—	—
I am an expert in one area of my field.	—	—

Now What?

As you review your answers to the questions above, what steps should you be taking to see that you really move on with your educational program? Part of the role of the Christian leader is to take leadership of himself or herself. What leadership do you need to exercise over yourself in this area?

For Further Consideration

Some of the newsletters that might help you as a Christian leader include:

Christian Leadership Letter, available upon request at no charge from World Vision International, 919ʹ W. Huntington Drive, Monrovia, California 91016. Much of the material in this book was taken from previous issues of this letter.

The Evangelical Newsletter attempts to give a synthesis of current religious events and thought from an evangelical perspective. It's available from The Evangelical Foundation, 1716 Spruce Street, Philadelphia, Pennsylvania 19103.

Context, edited by Martin E. Marty, is a bi-monthly reflection on Christian literature in the United States from the middle-of-the-road viewpoint. Marty does an excellent job of selecting and synthesizing.

Chronolog, available from Guidelines Publications, P.O. Box 456, Orinda, California 94563, is a monthly newsletter on time savers and managing your time which has a lot of management insight in it.

SEMINARS

There are many training seminars available, most of which are sponsored through the resources of your local university. The easiest way to learn about these is to place a telephone call to the nearest large university and ask for their industrial relations or management training center, and make inquiry as to how you can learn more. The seminars vary in cost and value, and it is usually a good idea to try to find someone who has been to one before.

World Vision International, 919 W. Huntington Drive, Monrovia, California 91016, sponsors two-day Managing Your Time seminars aimed primarily at Christian leaders. The first day deals with how to go about gaining mastery of your own personal time management. The second day of the two-day seminars tries to apply these personal concepts to the management of the Christian organization.

Yokefellow Institute, 920 Earlham Drive, Richmond, Indiana 47374, sponsors a number of workshops for pastors in a wide variety of subjects. Ask to be put on their mailing list.

Olan Hendrix's Management Skills Seminars, 150 S. Los Robles, Pasadena, California 91101, are three-day seminars which introduce the Christian executive to management concepts and also include a speed reading course.

Campus Crusade for Christ has week-long management seminars for pastors. Write to Mr. Steve Douglass, Arrowhead Springs, San Bernardino, California 92404, for information about whether they might be having a seminar in your area.

The Church Consultation Service, 177 N. Madison Avenue, Pasadena, California 91101, offers both regular and special training seminars.

Gil Peterson Associates, 18623 Brooke Ave., Arbor Vista, Grayslake, Illinois 60030, present "Creative Leadership in Management" and Christian Leadership Ministries. First is a series of one-, two-, or three-day management seminars for business and industry, presented from a Christian perspective and designed to meet the needs of individual organizations. Second is a program of twelve-hour Bible study skills and Bible teaching skills institutes designed for laity.

Institute for American Church Growth, 150 S. Los Robles, Suite 600, Pasadena, California 91101, directed by Win Arn, holds training seminars in church growth principles, has produced a series of films on church growth and publishes a magazine, *Church Growth: America.*

The Doctor of Ministry program of Fuller Theological Seminary, 125 N. Oakland Ave., Pasadena, California 91101, offers the highest level of church growth training available in its two-week seminars held in February on the Pasadena campus and in June in selected locations throughout the U.S. A limited number of auditors are accepted in each of the seminars.

Hagstrom Consulting, Inc., 83 Barrie Road, East Long Meadow, Massachusetts 01028, does seminars in the area of time management, solving "people problems," matching people's "strengths" with desired results, motivating, training and developing people, management "one on one"—setting objectives, reviews, and appraisals.

William Gast and Associates, 5230 Burgess Road, Colorado Springs, Colorado 80908, offer seminars on administrative systems for churches, charting for strength, living with membership turnover, motivation and introducing change.

American Society for Training and Development, P.O. Box 5307, Madison, Wisconsin 53705. Broad resource for people involved in aspects of training and management development.

Management Development Guide, American Management Association, 135 W. 50th Street, New York, N.Y. 10020, $3.75 per biannual copy, includes annuals about seminars and courses as well as AMA publications, media and customized programs in their professional and extension institute. Membership required.

CASSETTE TAPES

Even if you don't like to sit and listen to other people talk, portable cassette recorders make it possible for you to do two things at once. They are particularly useful while you are driving your car, waiting for others, or doing some manual work which doesn't require you to concentrate too heavily. There are a number of cassette series available:

Campus Crusade for Christ has a series of cassettes of varying quality. Write for their catalog. The ones by Howard Hendricks are particularly good. You might also be interested in the ones on management by Steve Douglass.

Word, Inc., Waco, Texas 76703, has a number of cassettes on management and leadership. Write for their catalog.

American Bible Society has the Bible recorded on tapes. Write them at 1865 Broadway, New York, N.Y. 10023.

Discipleship Tape Library is one of a number of libraries that makes tapes available at a nominal cost. Write for their tape catalog (435 West Boyd, Norman, Oklahoma 73069).

The Growing Church by C. Peter Wagner is a thirty-hour self-study course based on Donald McGavran's classic work, *Understanding Church Growth.* It contains McGavran's book, six cassette tapes by Wagner, and a 58-page workbook/study guide in a three-ring vinyl binder (Fuller Evangelistic Association, Box 989, Pasadena, California 91102).

Managing Time by Alec Mackenzie is available from Alec Mackenzie and Associates, Inc., P.O. Box 232, Greenwich, New York 12834. Nine cassettes and workbook published by Advanced Management Research, $295.

Time Management for the Secretary/Manager Team, by R. Alec Mackenzie with Billie Sorenson (Advanced Management Research, 1976), is a cassette program with an accompanying workbook. The nine cassette tapes contain much vital information for the secretary/manager team. The emphasis is on the team concept, with both people being responsible to one another through managing and protecting time for one another, communicating, setting and understanding goals, and learning together how to be more effective on the job. $295.

The School of World Mission at Fuller Theological Seminary, 135 N. Oakland Avenue, Pasadena, California 91101, has a number of its courses on tape. Write for their catalog.

You will also notice that there are many advertisements for management training tapes in both Christian and secular magazines. Be selective here. Choose the ones that seem to meet your needs.

MAGAZINES AND JOURNALS

Church Administration, published by the Southern Baptist Convention, is an outstanding publication that covers just what the title implies.

Search, published by the Southern Baptist Convention, is the scholarly publication with a distinct management thrust for the pastor, minister of education, and laity serving in leadership capacities.

Church Management: The Clergy Journal (115 N. Main Street,

Mount Holly, North Carolina 28120) covers a wide range of topics, mostly of interest to church business administrators.

Your Church: Its Planning, Building, Equipment, and Administration is available from the Religious Publishing House (122 Old York Road, Jenkintown, Pennsylvania 19406).

The Christian Ministry (407 S. Dearborn Street, Chicago, Illinois 60605) aims at providing the parish minister with a wide range of tools.

Harvard Business Review (Soldiers Field, Boston, Massachusetts 02163) is expensive, but well worth it for managers of large organizations who may want to keep abreast of advanced thinking in management in Western societies.

Business Week (published by McGraw-Hill, 1221 Avenue of the Americas, New York, N.Y. 10020) is a good magazine to keep abreast of what others are doing in the world of "getting things done." It is probably most useful for those managers who are involved in organizations which have quite a bit of interchange with secular organizations.

BOOKS

Look through the bibliography at the end of this book.

5 | You Are a Change Agent

MOST CHRISTIAN LEADERS are in the business of bringing about change. Almost by definition leadership involves movement. True, there are some settings in which the role of the leader is to maintain status quo, but even in this supposedly stable situation the leader has to somehow *change* (read, *quell*) any discontent that may come about because of the status quo!

Whether it be bringing about a program that has not been previously attempted in a local church, instituting a new training program in the youth ministry, or finding ways to reduce the cost of fund raising, the leader is in the business of changing things from the way they are to the way he or she perceives they ought to be.

It's a Good Thing to Recognize

It is extremely helpful for every leader to see himself or herself as an agent of change. To see oneself as a "change agent" rather than just a "manager" or an "administrator" is to push past all of the questions of what *skills are needed* by each of these roles to the question of *what new situation do we want to bring about,* or what are our goals for our organization?

Change Is Always Going On

In our Western society, and in the societies of developing countries, we are caught up in the ever-increasing pace of change.

We don't have to bring it about! It is going on all around us. Many times the change *we* need to bring about is to keep our organization abreast of the history flowing so quickly past us. If we see ourselves as *agents* of change, people who are attempting to direct history rather than be controlled by it, we will have better insight into how we can become more effective as Christian organizations and more useful servants of the One whom we call Lord.

The role of the change agent is to *identify needed directions* for the organization or the society, to help those involved *identify why such changes will benefit the organization,* to *strengthen the motivation* of those involved to move in appropriate directions, and to *enable people to bring about the change.*

One could probably define a leader or a manager using these same definitions of roles. The important ingredients here are the words *agent*—one who carries or brings something about—and *enable*—helping other people to do what they know needs to be done.

Organizations Tend toward Stability

Organizations in general, and Christian organizations in particular, tend toward stability. As we find more efficient ways of doing things, these tend to be codified into procedures. These procedures in turn quickly become "the way we do things around here." Efficiency almost always turns out to be the eventual enemy of effectiveness. As a consequence, we may become very contented with the *way* we are doing things, even though we may be quite discontented with the *results.*

Since most Christian organizations continue to exist because of the favorable perception of their supporters, rather than their necessary performance in the marketplace of life, it is all too easy for them to succumb to the idea that their lack of progress is God's will for them. One of the roles of the change agent is to help people see that God desires them to be growing, not only in their individual lives, but in the life of their organization. We should be quick to point out that in talking about organizational growth we are not really concerned with growth in numbers of people or growth in finances, but biblical growth in the relationship between individuals that results in the organization functioning like a human body rather than like a machine.

But, in almost every situation, the number of people in an organization who resist a particular change far outnumber those who are enthusiastic about it. As a consequence, to quote the words of Machiavelli, "There is nothing more difficult to carry out, nor more doubtful of success, nor more dangerous to handle than to initiate a new order of things." [1] The handling of change requires insight and skill.

How then do we begin? If we want to bring about change in an organization which apparently does not desire to change, how do we go about it? What do good change agents do?

Identify Needed Directions

In Chapter 14, "Planning As a Process," we will discuss ways and means of involving as many people as possible in the whole business of establishing organizational directions. Here we need to point out that if "you don't care where you're going, any road will take you there." Useful change demands that we have some vision of the future, some statement of faith about what we believe God would have us to do and to be. If the business of the manager and the change agent and the leader is to move the organization from the way things are "now" to the way things ideally should be in some future "then," it is necessary to discover the obstacles standing in the way of reaching that future. We must also identify some of the forces that will have an impact upon that future. The change that we want to bring about is to strengthen the positive and reduce the negative forces.

But assuming we know where we want to go and some of the things that might be needed to take us there, where do we begin?

Start with Discontent

Individuals only change when there is discontent. This may be a holy discontent or an unholy discontent, or it may be ethically neutral. It may be a *negative* discontent in the sense that people would like to see things done better than they are. Many times the change agent will first become aware of the need for change because of the expression of that discontent. At other times, the first role of the change agent is to identify areas of discontent and build on these. Saul Alinsky,[2] the famous union organizer,

---

[1] Niccolo di Bernado Machiavelli, *The Prince.*

[2] To better understand Saul Alinsky, read his *Rules for Radicals* (New York: Random House, Inc., 1972).

used to say, "Rub the bruises sore!" What was he saying? The same thing we are. Build on discontent that is already there. At first this may sound like meddling or causing dissension. Handled incorrectly it can very well be just that. On the other hand, a strong confrontation is sometimes needed to awaken everyone concerned to the need for change. Sometimes the sinner needs to be confronted with his sin!

Who Are the Opinion Leaders?

In every organization there will be those who, because of their position, or because of their personal influence, must be convinced of the need for change before it can be brought about. To attempt to steamroll new ideas past such individuals usually ends in disaster. The goal you are trying to accomplish must be owned by someone who has the capability and the power to bring it about.

Recognize that there is both a formal and an informal organization. A formal organization is easily recognized. The informal organization is much more difficult to understand. Like an iceberg, the organization has its formal tip which is highly visible and understandable, while underneath the water lies a much larger informal organization. As we have discussed elsewhere, the informal organization can include people who, because of their length of service with the organization, offices they have held in the past, or just by their sheer force of personality, have a great deal to do with the shaping of opinions within the organization.

Good Goals and Bad Goals

Eventually, everyone involved must believe this is a *good* goal because it is *our* goal. This is one of the major desires of the change agent. It says something, too, about the change agent's willingness to change himself or herself. We have no right to subject others to a process to which we are not willing to submit ourselves.

How do we go about making "my goal" into "our goal"? How do we bring about useful change?

Steps to Change

Take Your Time

It is true that sometimes a leader can move an entire organization just by the strength of his or her conviction and force of personality. However, too often the result is a feeling on the part of the organization that the people are working on the *leader's* goals rather than their own. So don't try to accomplish too much in too short a time. Keep your dreams big but your aim low. For example, you may see a need to consolidate your ministry, to eliminate some functions no longer needed. If you announce the addition or elimination of any ministry without taking the time to let the people involved come to their own conclusions about the worthiness of the move, you may meet a great deal of unnecessary and destructive opposition.

Find an Entry Point

For example, if you wanted to change the whole worship service in the local church to make it more meaningful to the current congregation, one entry point might be people's dissatisfaction with the organ. The occasion of finding a new organ might be used to bring about the changes in the worship service.

Involve As Many People As Possible

If you are contemplating a major change, find ways to let the people involved identify the need for change, as well as appropriate ways to bring it about. For example, you as a pastor may see the need to begin a satellite congregation or to offer a second Sunday morning service. What you have really identified is a need to permit more people to become a part of your local fellowship. By letting the appropriate boards and committees, or at times even the congregation, discuss first the need and second the possible or potential solutions, you will not only find goal owners, you may find a solution better than yours. This leads us to our next step:

Be Open to New Ideas

Means and methods are not as important as what it is you believe God wants accomplished. The role of the change agent is not necessarily to sell one idea, but to permit the group to discover a solution which is most appropriate for its skills. Again, we need to emphasize the need for goal ownership.

Break It Down into Steps

Don't try to carry off the whole program at once. Many times one cannot even share one's eventual dreams for what might be.

A number of commentators have observed that the church building boom which followed World War II gave many local congregations a great deal of confidence in their ability to get things
done. If they could build a building, they could also picture
themselves getting involved in a broader ministry. For example,
you might hope that one day you could institute a long-range
planning system within the organization that God could use to
give you better direction in your day-by-day decisions. However,
such an idea may be so foreign to the organization that it would
be much better to begin with the establishment of fairly short-
range goals and let people see the value of those first.

Build in Success

In your first attempts at doing something new, choose something that will have high visibility, of which most people will
approve, and about which people will feel they have a sense of
accomplishment.

Nothing succeeds like success. Machiavelli observed that people are lukewarm about things in which they have no experience,
but become real advocates of something they believe they can do.
Take the easy ones first. Let people experience the exhilaration of
accomplishing things together. Build in relationships. That's what
the body of Christ is all about. Make the goals "do-able," which
leads us to our next suggestion:

Affirm Progress

We need to stop and rejoice over the small victories. Too often
as leaders we keep pushing people forward without assuring
them that they really are succeeding. We can affirm success by
memos to appropriate people, by announcements in weekly or
monthly bulletins, by posters, bulletin boards, or special announcements—any way that seems appropriate. Realize, however, that to affirm progress you have to decide beforehand what
the indicators of progress are going to be. This is why what we
have said about breaking every task down into steps is important.
If, for example, there are five things that must be done to institute
a new procedure in an organization, try to use those milestones
not only as checkpoints to check up on people, but also to compliment them on having moved as well as they have.

Make Sure That Resources Are Adequate

This is always a test of faith, but if there is not some evidence that you have the physical and financial resources to carry off what is being proposed, people will usually sense this and approach the task half-heartedly. Another way of saying the same thing is, "Plan!" and if you discover that the plan you have made won't work, find another one.

In all of this, don't be afraid about the need for money. Money is the resource that we have to plan to find to carry out the task. Too often Christian organizations are controlled by their vision of how much money they can raise rather than their vision of what God wants them to do.

Revolution, Reform, or Innovation?

These are three ways of bringing about change. The first implies doing away with the old order, and complete rebuilding toward the new order. The second implies that there is something wrong with the existing order, that what we have done in the past is bad. Reformation is needed.

We favor the third method of change—innovation. Innovation seeks to cope with a future which is going to be different from the past by finding new ways to accomplish worthy goals. It does not stand in judgment of the past—it only recognizes that the future will probably be different.

However, people will usually identify a change agent as a revolutionary, a reformer, or an innovator. Make sure that you are correctly seen. If you look back over the steps to change which we have suggested in the previous paragraphs, you can see that failure at any one of these points might lead people to brand you as a revolutionary or a reformer, when actually you are trying to bring about an innovation.

For Further Reading

If you only have time for one book, get a copy of Lyle E. Schaller's book, *The Change Agent*. It is available in paper.

6 | Management Versus the Manager

HAVE YOU EVER FINISHED reading some beautifully written treatise on good management with a sigh of resignation, convinced that *you* will never be that kind of a person? Have you ever attended a two- or three-day seminar on good management practice and returned to your office only to discover that what seemed so clear in the classroom appears to be pretty fuzzy in practice? Well, rest assured that your experience is not uncommon. In fact, it is probably much more the rule than the exception. There is considerable difference between the overall *management theory* useful for framing our purposes and direction and the day-to-day business of managing (which one person has defined as "doing whatever is needed to get the job done").

Christian Organizations Need Good Management

Let us quickly state that we are all for good management. During the last one hundred years our technological society has demanded the development of people with special organizational skills, people who have a general theory of how organizations work best and what is needed to keep them moving toward their objectives. We give these people the general title of "Manager." This, we recognize, is almost a role unto itself. Perhaps the closest thing to it in the Bible is the gift of "helps," or administration. In the complex world in which most of us have been called to carry

51

out our part of God's program, we need to learn everything that modern management can teach us.

Management theory has to do with planning, organizing, directing, controlling, communicating, and a number of other functions required by modern organizations of almost any size.

That's Not What Happens in the Office

If you have ever had the experience of keeping an every-fifteen-minute record of everything you did for a week, you have probably discovered that you would be hesitant to submit your record as a good case study on sound managment. What managers *do* every day can best be described as leading, handling disturbances, acting as a figurehead, disseminating information, acting as a spokesperson, negotiating with people, monitoring how things are going, and allocating resources. Many of us feel that practically everything we do is in response to some problem. We see ourselves as continually fighting fires.

Managers Like It That Way

The interesting thing is that most managers like it that way. They enjoy the challenge of a new problem every hour or so, the ebb and flow of interruptions, the excitement of changed plans, new ideas. Oh, they would be very happy if they had more *time*. They picture themselves as stretched between conflicting values. They feel guilty about not spending more time with their families and working in their churches. They wish they could relax more. But when they do discover some better method of time management, more often than not they spend the time on doing more of the same.

Most managers picture themselves as never having enough information. Consequently, almost every decision they face depends upon internally processing whatever data they have with their own experience. Often managers describe the rationale for their final decisions as "hunch" or "feel."

Management versus the Manager

On the other hand, management theory is logical and rational. It seeks to anticipate the need it wants to fulfill—to describe the need and approaches to meeting it in factual terms. There is a rather tacit assumption that if all the data was available, the solution would be obvious. Essentially a problem-solving approach, it tends to avoid emotion and feeling, even though it recognizes that since it carries out its business through people, "people problems" will have to be dealt with.

The popular management theory of MBO (Management by Objective) is a good reflection of this rational thinking. Overall purposes are formulated by the leadership of the organization. Major objectives (goals) are then assigned to functional units. All of these goals are *future* events, or desirable futures, that the organization leadership believes would be advantageous in terms of outcome, be it money, product, service or even fellowship. The unit leader then sits down with key individuals and works out their personal objectives, which are, it is to be hoped, supportive of the organization's objectives. Performance against these objectives (desirable future events) is then the measurement used to manage the operation. Deviation from the anticipated goal is viewed as either a need to modify the plan ("corrective action") or modify the goal.

But the future seldom conforms to our desires, particularly in detail. There seems to be a much greater chance that something will go wrong than right. Consider the baseball batter as an example. His usual "plan" is to get on base, normally by hitting the ball with the bat. But baseball heroes are those who "fail" seven times out of ten; they bat .300. It is this unpredictability that challenges the manager. Most managers are attracted to management for this very reason.

What then of the theory? How does it relate to the practice?

Theory versus Practice

In an interesting article in the *Harvard Business Review* entitled, "Planning on the Left Side and Managing on the Right" (July/August 1976), Henry Mintzberg points out that the two hemispheres of the brain play different roles. The left side is the rational, linear side. It processes information bit-by-bit. The most obvious example is the left side's control of language. On the other hand, the right side appears to process all kinds of information simultaneously. It is the intuitive side, the place where a great deal of subconscious thought-process goes on. The title of Mintzberg's article is based on his suggestion that people who like to plan, to work things through logically, are probably predominantly "left-sided people," while people who act on hunch and intuition or with a considerable sense of the artistic are more "right-sided people."

Mintzberg's insight helps us to see that people who are good planners are not necessarily good managers, and people who do well at handling the everyday give-and-take of a typical hectic day may not be good planners.

To put it another way, it is one thing to be able to imagine the best of all worlds. It is quite another to have the ability to make that world come true. This comment neither downgrades the planners nor exalts the implementer. Both skills are needed, and both are found in many individuals.

The Big Picture versus the Snapshot

Management theory is extremely useful in carrying out any enterprise. Those of us involved in the leadership of Christian organizations ignore it to the peril of the enterprise for which we may be responsible. We need clearly stated purposes, well-conceived goals, detailed plans, methods of evaluation, and feedback. These are part of the big picture, the framework within which we have to operate.

But we also need *people* people, who, though they may be concerned with the big picture, are very much involved in the battle at hand. These people know that they are involved in an important and meaningful enterprise. But they also realize this: to achieve the ultimate purpose they are going to be faced with a myriad of everyday changes, decisions, frustrations, and hardships—the mortar that makes the grand edifice possible.

Three Kinds of Time

Earlier we introduced the idea that the manager of the smaller agency or church, or the middle manager of the larger enterprise, has three kinds of time: *superior time, peer and subordinate time,* and *discretionary time.* As far as the organizational life is concerned, he/she has little or no control over the time he/she spends with his/her superior. One may have more control over the amount of time spent with peers and subordinates, but many times this is built into the organizational style. Whatever time is left in the course of a day or week can be used at one's discretion. If peers and subordinates don't spend time in giving thought to the future (planning), one will not have that opportunity during that block of time. If one's superior does not set aside planning time, one will be able to do little about it. It is only in our *discretionary* time, the time directly under our control, that we as leaders can devote time to the kind of reflection necessary to give us the big picture that we need to intuitively ("right side"!) process the data we have when we are faced with those daily fires.

Levels of Discretionary Time

Management theory recognizes this dilemma when it pictures the senior executive as spending a good deal of time in long-range planning, policy decisions, and giving general guidance to the ship. First-level managers are recognized to have very little time to carry out this function. "Middle managers" fall somewhere in between. Whether you seem to be fighting too many fires or too few depends on where you are in the organizational structure. People at the head of an organization *should* (!) have more discretionary time than others further down (see Chapter 19, "A Matter of Size").

Where Are You?

There are many levels of management, varying from the small church with only one staff person to the large denomination or agency with hundreds of paid staff and thousands of volunteers. Place yourself somewhere on the scale from little overall responsibility to maximum. This gives you some insight into how much time should be spent on the management theory and how much should be spent on actual managing.

If you are a "left-sided" person, one who likes to do the thinking and the planning, look for someone who is more on the "right side," the everyday firefighting kind of person, to help you. If you are spending all your time in the midst of the fray, see what can be done to set aside time for some praying and contemplating about the future—this business we call planning (really making statements of faith about what you believe God wants your organization to be).

Don't get hung up on the fact that every day does not go according to plan or that you are not the best time manager in the world. On the other hand, dip into the literature that deals with technique (as opposed to theory) of what is best described as "time management." A great deal has been learned about how to more effectively handle mail, interruptions, visitors, meetings, memos, conflict, and a host of other experiences that you will encounter every day.

It's a Process

This is one of our favorite phrases, but we think it goes along with the idea that Christians are *becoming* people. We don't learn to be good leaders or good managers overnight. Similarly, as the situation changes we, too, have to change, which means that we're going to have to be involved in the kind of continuous education we described in the previous chapter.

For Further Reading

The Effective Executive by Peter F. Drucker is one of the best. Drucker is the recognized dean of management trainers. This book is designed to help the individual improve his insights into people and helping others achieve their goals while achieving his own. Hardcover.

The Time Trap: Managing Your Way Out by Alec Mackenzie begins with the problem of managing yourself as a key to managing your time. MacKenzie has an excellent section on working with your secretary. Hardcover and paperback.

7

You As
a
Young Leader

BOTH OF US ARE at that point in life where we feel comfortable looking back down the road we have traveled. It has been an exciting life. If we had to do it again, we would—gladly. Perhaps we should have taken more time to smell the flowers and listen to the birds singing along the way, but the tasks, responsibilities, and opportunities have been fulfilling. Many men and women have been our teachers. We are grateful to them all. For those of you who are beginning this exciting journey, or have the opportunity to counsel young leaders, these seem to be among the things that stand out as important to us:

School and Society

Each of us is the product of our parents, our school, and our society. This is so obvious as to be forgotten in most instances. Of these three, we would like to focus on the impact of our schooling and our society, our culture, upon us.

We in the "Western" part of our world are the most schooled of all people. We recognize that a high percentage of our readers have had sixteen years of school, many much more. Our society handles this long period of schooling with the (hidden) idea of postponed adulthood. A man or a woman is only considered an adult when he or she has left school and taken a full-time job. Even if he or she is married, in the classroom and the school one is still treated as preadult.

This you-are-not-an-adult conditioning elicits the expected result: men and women in school typically don't *act* like adults. It's amazing how many young *adults,* who in three weeks will graduate from seminary to accept a pastorate, live out the same rituals of dress, horseplay, and college humor. There is much talk about the heavy grind of college and graduate study. Three months later all this is left behind, and the new Christian leader is wondering how he even thought that forty hours a week of classes and study could have been a hardship.

The result of this postponed adulthood and its accompanying structured school life is a naïveté about how difficult the task of leadership really is. Since many of us have not yet had the *experience* of managing ourselves, we have little insight into how to manage others.

The Public and Private Sectors

We are also living in a society that increasingly lives a compartmentalized life, dividing it primarily into private and public sectors. What we do "on the job" is differentiated from what we do with "our own time." This is a natural response to an increasingly complex society. As time seems to compress itself and the number of new things to be learned or handled multiplies, we long to find some place to hide, a place to hang loose and "be ourselves."

The result is that life becomes more and more fractured. The pressures of society push us to compartmentalize life. To use the technological skills we have mastered to earn a living seems cold and mechanical. "Do not fold, staple or spindle," we cry. The difficulty is that we quickly set the different compartments one against the other.

The Christian is unique. He or she believes that there is ultimate purpose and meaning to life: "The chief end of man [and woman] is to give glory to God and enjoy him forever." As Christian leaders we need to bring our relationships into our task. We need to strive for integration, for wholeness.

The Normal Phases of Adult Life

In her book, *Passages,*[1] Gail Sheehy points out that there are normal phases of adult life quite as distinct as the normal phases of childhood. We move from one phase to another in a series

[1] Gail Sheehy, *Passages* (New York: E. P. Dutton & Co., Inc., 1976).

of "passages." People are different at differing times in their lives. They do respond differently, see things differently, at different ages.

When we are young, we *refuse* to compromise. As we grow older, we realize we *have* to compromise. Perhaps in our thirties, we *learn* to compromise. By forty, we are *willing* to compromise. Sometime in life we (it is to be hoped) learn that compromise is what life is all about. We learn that often our "ideals" were less than ideal when placed alongside those of others. "*Our* goals" turn out to be more desirable than "*my* goals."

The idealism of youth is the bedrock on which the wisdom of maturity is built. Nothing wrong with that. But age does make a difference. The young Christian leader may not experience this, but it needs to be respected in others.

Paradox

Our society is oriented toward solutions. Our technological advancement gives the illusion that we have much more control over destinies than we actually have. Too often young Christians fail to live in the light of the paradoxes of life so clearly stated in the Bible. The ultimate paradox, of course, is God's sovereignty and our freedom. Both are true. God is sovereign. His will *will* be done. Yet, men and women are free. We are responsible. "Logic" says those two ideas cannot coexist. Maturity discovers that we can live and work as though both were true.

Learn early to live in the light of faith.

Courage

To exercise good leadership is not easy. To assume a position of leadership often isolates one. There comes a time when *you* must decide, often for an unpopular position. So it takes courage.

But it is easy to confuse courage with dogmatism, an unwillingness to listen or to bend. Single-mindedness can lead to narrowmindedness. In his book, *The Courage to Create*,[2] Rollo May points out that it doesn't take a great deal of courage to move ahead on something in which you have complete confidence. True courage moves ahead in full knowledge that failure is possible.

---

[2] Rollo May, *The Courage to Create* (New York: W. W. Norton & Company, Inc., 1975).

Love

Jesus tells us that the basic test of our commitment to him is our love for one another (John 13: 35). Love has to do with relationships. There are some people who are so consumed with tasks and accomplishment, that they have little time for relationships. But love, without focus, without shared purpose, can become ingrown.

Love with abandon, but love with purpose.

Education

Your education has just begun. Ahead lies the "School of Hard Knocks." But for the effective leader of the future there will also be more, and often continuous, training. Build it into your goals.

Almost everyone is surprised by that first job after leaving school. No matter how well the organization explained it, the position seldom is what we expected. Time and again recent seminary graduates have complained, "I'm not using 10 percent of what I learned!" Be patient. You will. Not all of it, but a great deal. A good education teaches us how to *learn*. Once that is mastered, the whole world opens up.

Again the paradox: the more we learn, the more humbled we are at our own ignorance. And yet, with this comes a sense of completeness. Count on it.

Learn from Your Seniors

All of us have so very much to learn from others. Young executives need to recognize that there are few things more valuable than the experience we gain and garner in living our lives. Find ways to spend time with those who have been down the road a bit farther and who know something of the pitfalls as well as the "freeways" which can be traversed. Don't be afraid to ask for counsel and advice (older colleagues are almost always happy to give it!). Find ways to seek out time with your superiors and others who have moved on ahead; their counsel and advice can be tremendously profitable and oftentimes extremely redemptive.

Watch for Models

How grateful we can be that the Word of God has provided us with various models for living, most perfectly exemplified in the model of our Lord Jesus Christ. In our ministries we need to look for models among our colleagues and fellow staff members. We believe the apostle Paul had this in mind when he wrote, "Agree together, my friends, to follow my example. You have us for a model; watch those whose way of life conforms to it" (Phil. 3: 17, NEB). Those of us in leadership positions have a special opportunity—and a special responsibility—to point others, through our example, toward greater fruitfulness and deeper commitment to our Lord. Our organizations ought also to seek to model for others. In our particular ministry, we constantly remind ourselves that we should strive to be examples of Christian excellence as leaders of other Christian organizations visit us to find out about our management systems, procedures, and policies. Our role as models—whether on a personal or organizational level—should never be reason for pride, but rather, for profound gratitude. We should watch for models and learn all we can from what they have to show us in behavior, actions, and attitude.

Be a Reader

Be as widely read in as many disciplines as you possibly can. If you don't enjoy reading, cultivate the habit. Read contemporary literature; read literature that pertains to your area of concern and work; read much in the area of devotional materials; read management and leadership books and articles. Build shelves in your library for devotional material, reference material, management and leadership material, and other particular disciplines and interests that you may have. Read! It is one of the best ways to grow!

Learn from Failure

We need to recognize that in what we often call failure, we can learn the very most. Most failures can and ought to be learning situations. There is nothing wrong in failing or in making a mistake. Let's just be certain that we don't make the same mistakes twice or three times, and thus fail for the same reason. When you fail, pick yourself up, dust yourself off, and move ahead to build upon the experience. Don't bemoan the fact of failure, but ask the Lord to again use this experience redemptively in your life and ministry.

Purpose

Christian leadership demands a purpose. Under the Lordship of Christ, we need to decide why we are here and where we are going. Doubts will come. In a world where the chances of things going wrong far exceed the likelihood of things going right, we can easily resign ourselves to failure. That is why we must continually reaffirm our purpose.

Prayer

Who can explain it? We have direct access to the Maker of the universe. He has gone before and follows behind. Call on him. Counsel with him. In his Word, God continually invites us into his presence: "Call unto me. . . ."; "We have an advocate with the Father, Jesus Christ the righteous" (Jer. 33: 3; 1 John 2: 1). God's way of working is in answer to believing prayer!

Believe

Ours is the God who is *for* us! He is not playing games. Daily trust your life to him. "The steps of a good man [woman] are ordered by the Lord" (Ps. 37: 23 KJV). One of us has Psalm 32: 8 as his life verse: "I will instruct you and teach you the way you should go; I will counsel you with my eye upon you." Try it; it works!

For Further Reading

A book we often recommend for young people starting out in their careers is *What Color Is Your Parachute?* by Richard Nelson Bolles. The thrust of this book is that the best way to find the right job is to research the one you want and then go after a specific job. Read the book—it's very helpful.

8 | When It's Time to Retire

ONE OF THE FACTS OF LIFE in the Western world is retirement—the idea that at some particular time or age a person should leave his or her vocational or organizational responsibilities and "retire." Fifty years ago many people looked upon retirement as one of the goals of life. At the time it was seen as a just reward for a long and hard career. Visions of quiet days idled away by gentle streams or pleasant vistas were seen as very alluring.

Now the reality of senior citizenhood has set in. In 1977, 9.7 percent of the U.S. population was over 65. Senior citizens are now recognizing that they are the largest "minority" in the country. Not all of them are pleased with the way they are being treated.

Whether you are beginning to contemplate retirement yourself, or whether you are a Christian executive who needs to help other people prepare for retirement, there is much more to the process than at first meets the eye. What you might have considered as primarily a question of finances or retirement plans turns out to be one of life's greatest transitions for many people.

We would like to consider retirement from the perspective of its impact on the individual and steps we might take to make the transition an effective one.

All of our advertising keeps bombarding us with the idea that to be young is good and to be old is bad. If the same form of advertising was applied to the idea that to be white is good and to be black is bad, civil rights advocates would rise up in indig-

64 YOU AND YOURSELF

nation all over the country. Perhaps one day the Gray Panthers will have their way with the media! Meanwhile, better face it, the emphasis on youth is probably not going to go away very soon.

Our society continually tries to brainwash itself to avoid the fact of death. Rather than death being viewed as a final climax to the productive life and an entrance into the presence of the King, death is seen as something to be avoided and glossed over. Old people are viewed as a sign of approaching death. Many people avoid them.[1]

We are just now beginning to realize that our transportation systems and our service industries are geared to younger people. Senior groups are beginning effective campaigns to change this.

The Organizational Security Blanket

Few of us recognize the sizeable feeling of security we gain from working within an organization.

First, it gives us a sense of place. We know who we are. We know where we fit. Have you ever noticed how people tend to introduce you? "I'd like you to meet Mr. Brown. He's with Christian Life International."

Second, it gives us leverage in the world. The organization will stand behind us in terms of credit ratings, social support (such things as life insurance and other fringe benefits), and in a host of other ways which we might never think of (passes to certain functions, an ability to travel, expense accounts, and so forth). When was the last time you combined a business meeting or trip with a social event?

Third, organizations give us a goal orientation. We share a common task with others in which we have a common responsibility and for which we feel a common drive. This gives us something to look forward to, as well as a feeling of accomplishment.

Fourth, a role in an organization gives us prestige, not only with our neighbors, but with ourselves. It's nice to know this building, this project, these people are what they are because of what we have been able to do (even with the Lord's help!).

Fifth, organizations give us an opportunity to help others, to feel responsible, to feel that we are needed.

---

[1] In his book, *The Denial of Death* (New York: Free Press, 1973), Ernest Becker does an excellent job of demonstrating that most of life's actions center around denial of our mortality.

. Sixth, organizations permit us to relate as professionals to others. A pastor will naturally join a pastoral association. The Christian executive will look to others in a similar field, people with whom he/she can exchange information or with whom he/she may join a technical society.

The day you retire from an organization many of these things are removed. Now you are one individual "against the world." Your mobility may be greatly reduced, your sense of direction may be gone. Your feeling of self-worth may be greatly diminished.

Be Prepared

How do we cope with such a radical change? The first thing to do is to recognize that it does lie ahead. Be prepared.

In many ways, preparing for retirement is much like preparing to enter a new business. This is particularly true for the individual who has worked as part of a large organization. There are a whole list of questions to be faced:

1. What will you do for the remaining years of your life?
2. Where will you live?
3. What will be your relationships with your children?
4. What kind of environment should you be in?
5. What kind of life style would you like to have?
6. What kind of life style will you probably be forced to have? What will be your standard of living?
7. Can it (retirement) be postponed?
8. Can it be hastened?

Notice how many of these questions are similar to those we asked in the chapter, "You and Your Job." Both are an attempt to anticipate the kind of future we would like to have, to take the steps that will move us in that direction.

Have a Goal!

One of the most deadly enemies of life is a lack of purpose. Too many people set a goal to *begin* retirement, but no goal as to what they will accomplish or become as a result of retirement. Goals are powerful motivators. At 63 we need goals for 70. At 68 we need goals for 75.

Is there a book that you've always wanted to write? By beginning to gather background information on it and putting it aside while you're yet an active member of an organization, you will have a head start when you finally have the time to do the writing. Is there a new skill that you wanted to acquire one day "when you had the time"? Start doing research now on what schools might be available. You are going to be a different person than you are now. Although in many ways you are going to have physical limitations you did not have when you were younger, in other ways you will have experiences and capabilities to make you much more "valuable." Where do all of these changes fit?

Solutions

View this as a career change. In the same way that you would investigate your potential role in a new organization, investigate this new role you're going to play in society.

Consider what God has made you, what he has allowed you to become. If, as a Christian, you view your chief purpose to bring glory to him, what is it he has taught you about yourself, others, and the world, that you might now use in some new and fresh way?

Analyze your life style and standard of living; what is there about your present life style sustained by the fact that you work for an organization? What part of it will have to change? What are your likes and dislikes? Perhaps you'll discover that there are a number of penalties to working in your present situation which may disappear when you retire. Perhaps you will have new interests. You may want to consider visiting the local university to take something like the Strong Aptitude Test which would give you some additional insight into things you would really like to do.

Plan financially. Many life insurance companies will help you work through an analysis of your situation and then give you a picture of the possibilities of having the kind of future *financially* you would like to have. Their objective, of course, is to sell life insurance, but it is worth the effort to begin to ask yourself some questions as to the level of income you expect to live on and whether any retirement plan that your organization has, plus social security, plus whatever other financial resources you have are going to be adequate. Investigate the many savings plans and retirement accounts available for self-employed people or for wives, plans that help you to postpone income tax costs until you are in a lower tax bracket.

This may also have something to say about your learning to be a manager of money. It's surprising how many of us who have been working on a salary all of our lives have really become used to letting our salaries control our expenses. Even men and women who do an excellent job of managing the finances of their companies often are poor personal finance managers. Perhaps you need to get some outside consulting help here.

Plan for it just as you would plan for entering your own business, for in one sense that is what you're doing. One solution many people have found worthwhile is to launch their own business. Perhaps there is a business you can start now, even while you are still working for the organization from which you will retire. This should be openly discussed by all concerned.

Try to "test it out" or prepare for it before it happens. Both the individual and the organization should consider ways of gradual transition rather than an abrupt change. For example, if you were going to get involved in your own business, perhaps you should gain your organization's permission (if needed) to start experimenting with a business like this now. Most businesses, crafts or hobbies have their own newsletters and journals. Go to the local library and find out what they are and then start subscribing to them.

Build bridges for the future by planning how the skills you now have and will have in the future may be used by others. Take some of the aptitude tests and other tests available to help you discover your particular talents and what you like to do. You may be amazed at the possibilities of a whole new career. Don't overlook the possibility of doing consulting for other organizations similar to yours. This could be accomplished either by short-term visits or with perhaps two to three months spent as an enabler or facilitator. The latter role is particularly useful in assisting other local church congregations.

Build up contacts and friendships for the type of life you are going to lead. If you are thinking of moving into a retirement community, develop friendships with people living in such places. Find out the pros and cons. If you are a person who has always enjoyed being with people younger than yourself, perhaps you will find it distressing to join the ranks of "senior citizens." On the other hand, many people enjoy the company of people their own age. Some people advocate moving into a retirement community even before one retires so that one can begin to establish lasting friendships. Many times people who postpone leaving the home they had lived in for many years find it increasingly difficult as the years go by.

The Advantages of Age

Old age has a lot of things going for it: wisdom about the world and how things work, a broad knowledge of its different aspects, the "experience" of having made mistakes, a greater tolerance for others which results in a greater ability to love and understand. Many people become more patient as they grow older, although it is a well-known phenomenon that as we approach the end of life, we tend to exhibit many of the personality traits we may have covered up during early and mid-life.

Weigh the advantages of advancing years. Your lifetime of experience may be exactly what's needed to move another person along the road of increased effectiveness.

The Role of the Christian Organization

Most Christians do respect the wisdom that comes with years, so at least we have some advantage over the non-Christian. However, as a Christian executive responsible for people who are approaching retirement in your organization, how much can be done to pave the way, so that "retirement" becomes a milestone along the way and not the entrance to nonpersonhood?

First, and most obvious, is the need for assistance in financial planning. An organization can take the lead in helping its staff think through their financial situations and to the extent that is possible, provide them with a retirement plan to meet their needs. It is surprising how many Christian organizations have retirement plans about which the employee can only learn with a great deal of digging. Any retirement plan should give the staff member a yearly report on his or her anticipated income at the time of retirement.

Second, provide awareness of the problems of retirement. It is all too easy to lull ourselves to sleep by imagining how great it's going to be not to *have* to work, rather than to realize that work is at the very core of life.

Third, consider retirement education, starting no later than five years before the mandatory age for retirement within your organization. This might take the form of encouraging staff members to take applicable courses in nearby schools, to provide them with literature from some of the senior citizens' societies like the American Association of Retired Persons.

Fourth, consider ways of continuing to employ key people who have passed the mandatory retirement age. There are a number of ways to do this. Many seminaries renew the contract with their faculty on a year-by-year basis. Others find new consultative assignments for their retirees, many times rehiring the individual as a consultant. If it fits in with the plans of the employee, many times there will be specific assignments he/she can continue to do on a part-time basis.

Fifth, consider whether mandatory retirement is really to the advantage of your organization. There is a good deal of discussion about this subject, and we realize that there are many pros and cons. Some people feel that older people need to be moved along to make room for younger people. Contrariwise, a growing organization often needs all the mature leadership it can find.

Sixth, make sure you are not building a financial trap for your staff in the name of Christian commitment. For example, most churches now realize that by giving their pastor a manse, they have kept him or her from accumulating equity in a home for retirement years. If low salaries are part and parcel of your organizational structure, then perhaps you need to consider a retirement program that provides an unusually high percentage of retirement income.

For Further Reading

Paul Tournier's *Learn to Grow Old* is very helpful.

See your local library for the wide range of books written on things you can do after you retire.

9	# The Price of Leadership [1]

TRUE LEADERSHIP, even when it is practiced by the most mature and emotionally stable person, always exacts a toll on the individual. In our world it seems to be axiomatic that the greater the achievement, the higher the price to be paid. The same is true of leadership. Jesus himself seemed to have this thought in mind when he said, "Whoever would save his life will lose it, and whoever loses his life for my sake, he will save it" (Luke 9: 24).

It is so very true that any worthwhile accomplishment has a price tag on it. The issue reduces itself to one basic question: how much are you really willing to pay—in hard work and sweat, in patience, in faith and endurance—to obtain it?

Ted Williams—baseball superstar of the forties and fifties—was once asked about his natural ability and immediately replied, "There is no such thing as a natural born hitter. I became a good hitter because I paid the price of constant practice, constant practice." Likewise, professional excellence in leadership doesn't just happen; it comes only through persistent effort.

Criticism

Criticism is a great price paid by leaders. If one cannot handle criticism, it means that basically he or she is emotionally immature. This defect will eventually show up and impede the

---

[1] Much of the material in this chapter was adapted from *The Making of a Christian Leader* by Ted Engstrom (Grand Rapids: Zondervan Publishing House, 1976), and is used by permission.

leader's and the group's progress toward the common goal. Every leader has to expect some criticism.

The mature leader is able to handle this and makes the needed personal adjustments and corrections. He or she is able to say, in essence, "Thank you for your criticism of my life. It has led me to a deeper self-examination, which I needed."

Fatigue

Someone has said that the world is run by tired men. There is probably real substance in the statement, for genuine leaders must be willing to rise early and study longer than their contemporaries.

A wise leader will try to find a balance, a change of pace to reduce stress. You have no doubt heard the cliché, "I'd rather burn out for God than rust out for the devil." That sounds noble and pious, and a person's dedication must come close to the tenor of the thought.

But if a person "burns out" completely, that person's influence and contribution end. Proper health care, rest, and balance will help a leader maintain the ability to persist. A leader must be prepared to recognize the cost of leadership, both emotionally and physically.

Time to Think

Another price paid by Christian leaders is the time that must be taken for creative thinking and meditation. We do not often think of this as a price to pay, but it is. Most people are too busy to take time to really think.

For the sake of an objective, many leaders want to surge ahead without paying the price of thinking it through to determine the best methodology to meet the goal. It is well said that "the solution is not to work harder, but to work smarter."

Loneliness

A third price the leader has to pay—one we seldom consider —is the willingness to be alone because personal freedom has been lost in the service of others. A true leader promotes others— their interests, values, and goals. At the same time, the effective leader must strive to fulfill personal potential and goals without being absorbed into the group. This leaves him/her living alone, somewhere in between, because he/she has to both identify with and be isolated from people.

The leader must be able to welcome friendship, but he/she has to be mature enough and have enough inner strength to stand alone against opposition.

Identification

Not only must the leader be alone and isolated at times, but paradoxically he/she must also identify with the group. The leader must always remain ahead of the group, but simultaneously walk with the people. This can be a fine line. There must be some distance between leader and followers. It is vital that the leader recognize this principle, yet be able to relate to associates.

This means there must be willingness to be an open, honest human being. Humanness has to come through. The leader cannot be seen as a robot, a cold, mechanical person afraid of letting the true self emerge.

To identify with people, leaders must pay the price of taking time to know their people—to share in their emotions, victories, and defeats. Since most goals cannot be reached in isolation, the group must be leaned upon. The leader has to be aware of the group-mind, be willing to make concessions, and lead graciously without losing sight of the long-range objective.

Make Unpleasant Decisions

Many times it becomes the duty of an effective leader to remove someone who is not performing up to the stated standard. Christian organizations often have trouble at this point because leaders are naturally loathe to hurt people.

All leaders must be willing to pay this price for the sake of the whole. It is not easy, especially when one desires approval from everyone.

In most cases, when a person is relieved because of unsatisfactory performance, we are actually helping him or her; when the person is inadequate on a job, he/she is slowly being destroyed inside by the pressure and strain. Secretly he/she may be praying for deliverance!

Competition

Still another peril of leadership is the effect of competition. There is a price for leaders to pay if they suffer from a "competition anxiety" that takes the form of either the fear of failure or of success.

The fear of failure stifles competition because the leader will be afraid to proceed or become too involved; achievement is curtailed, and a loss of identity is sustained. To overcome this anxiety, the leader must do some serious reality-testing to know what the competitive world really is.

The fear of success can be just as crippling. The leader may appear to be well-adjusted, outgoing, and extroverted, but the price paid by an organization with such people is very high. A leader with this kind of neurosis will develop increasing guilt feelings as he or she and the organization achieve. This kind of person may strive hard, but will usually falter before the actual achievement. He/she will often find some excuse (which to him/her is perfectly logical) to block the realization of the ultimate goal.

Abuse of Power

In the long history of mankind, power has become accepted as a basic characteristic of leadership. In any organization, including a Christian group, when a person is given authority he or she is in a legitimate position to exercise control and influence. For some people this is ego-building, and leads to autocracy. It is a peril, and there is a price to pay to keep from falling prey to this insidious temptation.

False Pride and Jealousy

False pride and jealousy are twins. Popularity can affect a leader's performance. Feelings of infallibility and indispensability can decrease effectiveness. And it is not uncommon for leaders to go through deep depression.

Every person must have some pride. But pride turns to egotism when we magnify ourselves to the point at which we have no place for the other person. It is false pride when we become so wrapped up in ourselves that other people count for little. This kind of pride or egotism is far different from having a healthy self-concept.

We all desire to be popular, and there is no great virtue in being unpopular. But there must be balance. A leader should be respected and held in esteem to get the job done better, but popularity can be purchased at too high a price.

When the price of humility is not paid, the temptations of infallibility and indispensability lurk. When people have false pride, it is easy to accept the rationalization that they are less liable to make mistakes than others. Unless a person perceives his/her true self-worth and is led by the Holy Spirit, he/she may easily fall into this subtle trap. Despite experience and maturity, leaders often fail to see that all of us are prone to make mistakes. "After all, my judgment has usually proved accurate," is what many reply.

The myth of indispensability is often perpetuated by the best-intentioned people. Frequently organizations face this with their older leaders, who become progressively less able with age to assess their contributions objectively. They may drag their heels and really unconsciously hinder—or at least retard—growth and development.

Utilization of Time

Of all the things we have to work with, the most important is the time God has given to us. There is a price to pay in the use of our time because it seems that we human beings are born congenitally lazy. So we have to alter this process.

In the final analysis, managing our time really means managing ourselves. We have to budget our time just as carefully as we must budget our money.

Rejection

A leader, especially a Christian, must also be ready to pay the price of personal rejection. There is always the strong possibility that somewhere he or she may be maligned for his/her faith or Christian perspective on issues. This was the path Jesus walked: "He came to his own home, but his own people received him not" (John 1:11).

The leader must be able at times to resist praise. He/she must have the courage to stand up against the spirit of the age. The leader must put the praise of God above the praise of men. He/she knows that "the fear of man lays a snare" (Prov. 29:25). The verdicts or judgments of men do not change one's standard if it is truly God- and people-oriented.

It takes a person with good ego strength to be able to cope with rejection. Normal, well-adjusted people want to be liked;

it can become a difficult road to walk if a leader feels the cooling winds of indifference or dislike. Often people who are rejected are not recognized for their strength until they have left or died. Monuments are then built with the stones once thrown at the person in life. This is not easy to accept, but the leader must be prepared emotionally and spiritually to face this possibility.

You may be able to think of other ways in which a true leader must be ready to pay a price if he or she is to retain a responsible position. When all is said and done, when there is a willingness to make the sacrifices necessary for success, the span of service will be marked by high quality and excellence.

For Further Reading

The Making of a Christian Leader by Ted W. Engstrom is a distillation of one Christian leader's thirty-five years of experience leading Christian organizations. The book covers the whole spectrum of leadership from the biblical basis to the roles and activities of the Christian leader. Hardcover and paper.

Spiritual Leadership by J. Oswald Sanders has had a profound effect on many Christian leaders. It deals with the spiritual dimension of the leader's life. Paperback.

So You Want to Be a Leader by Kenneth Gangel is an excellent book on leadership from a Christian perspective. Paperback.

Part II

You
and
Others

10 You and Your Leader

HOW OFTEN WE DESCRIBE people as "fitting in," either very well or not so well. What we mean is that they view their fellow employees and are viewed by them as doing their assigned job and being emotionally and physically supportive of others.

What makes a person "fit in"? There are obviously many factors: skill, personality, and experience among them. But a great deal depends on whether he or she sees himself as relating to an organization or an individual. We join organizations. We work for and with people.

Making a Success Out of Your Boss

Interpreting and acting on what your superior wants and needs, rather than what you believe the organization wants and needs, has some extremely practical and important consequences. First, it keeps the lines of responsibility clear. Second, it makes communication much simpler. Third, it keeps loyalties from becoming divided. The result is a much more effective organization and much happier staff members.

Our immediate response to the idea of "my boss first, my organization next" might be, "What if he or she is a bum? What if he or she is acting unethically?" That's easy. Get a new boss! "How?" Leave the organization if you have to. But if it is not a question of ethics, then do everything you can to make him or her effective.

How Do You Make Your Boss a Success?

Represent your boss fairly. He or she is also human. He is bound to have weaknesses and shortcomings. Talk about his abilities and try not to discuss his/her weaknesses.

Try to understand your boss. What's her style? People are different. How does she think? *Why* does she think that way? What does she do best? Is she a decision maker, a problem solver, or both?

Try to do it your boss's way, even if your way seems better. One day she'll discover your way.

Keep him informed. Don't surprise him. Tell him/her first about the decision you want made, next what problems you anticipate, and above all, what you plan to do.

Give her alternatives. If you are asking for a decision, don't give her an alternative of one. Think through acceptable alternatives. You'll be less disappointed and so will she.

What about "Company Loyalty"?

Haven't military organizations like the Marines done a good job of building *esprit de corps* through "loyalty to the outfit"? What about pride in the organization?

There is little doubt that some organizations have developed a high degree of pride in their present and past accomplishments and/or methods of operations. But such pride is especially the result of teamwork, and it becomes a spur toward greater cross-commitment rather than a detriment to it.

What about Volunteer Organizations?

Does this apply to the local church? We believe that it does. Too often the local church organization (committee, board, commission) is wrapped up in what it does, its activities, rather than its goals. The volunteer may not describe the group leader in the same terms as his supervisor at work, but his concern for him or her should be even greater.

Does This Leave Any Room for Criticism?

Personal commitment is a three-way street: up, down, sideways. When we treat others as persons of worth, they usually respond in kind. This in turn produces a climate within which constructive change can take place.

Have you been working just for the organization? Try working for your boss. You may like it.

Information Is a Key to Good Relationships

One of the least understood aspects of management communication is that of giving your superior the information he or she needs to function effectively. (It follows that your subordinates have the same difficulty with you.) Many Christian executives are just not getting the kind of data they need to do the Lord's work effectively.

The Activity Report

Most organizations of any size or age have recognized the need for written reports. Unfortunately, too many "activity" or "progress" reports are of minimum value because they limit themselves to information about things over which we have the least control—*the past*. By the time the report has been read, the deed is done. If things are going in a way other than what was expected, all that can be done is to correct past errors or change previous decisions. Surely, every executive wants to know what has happened. But if he or she is to operate as an executive, the *last* thing one needs to know is what has happened.

What Your Leader Wants to Know

The first thing your *leader* wants to know is *what decisions do you want him or her to make.* This is the primary role of the executive—to choose between alternatives, to make decisions.

Now it can be argued that if the executive has all the data, he or she can decide what decisions should be made. This may be sometimes true for the supervisor at the lowest level of management. But the person we are considering here is one who has other executives working for him or her, a person like *you*. Part of your job is first to recognize when a decision is needed and second, at what level it should be made.

Your identification of needed decisions and your recognition that these decisions should be made at a higher level in the organization is both a measure of your own ability and an indication of how your superior can help.

It is helpful here to recognize the different *levels* of delegation that exist. Too many people think delegation means no longer having any control of a situation. But seldom do we delegate everything. Consider these levels of delegation:

Level 1:   Do it and don't report back.
Level 2:   Do it and report back immediately.
Level 3:   Do it and report back routinely.
Level 4:   Investigate and make recommendations to me and we will decide together.
Level 5:   Gather data for me and I will decide.

It is important that you understand these differences. You and your superior will want to use different levels at different times and for different projects. This is obvious. But it may not be obvious to the people you are working with.

Many times an executive fails to make a decision because no one called to his or her attention the fact that there was a decision to be made. The problem may well have been that the one who did make the decision didn't realize that he was not supposed to make it. He thought that authority had been delegated to him.

Decisions are like prayer. We can't get involved if we don't know a need exists. One of our standard instructions to the people who work for us is, "Don't surprise me!"

The Second Most Important Thing

. . . is *what problems you are facing*. Here again you are bringing to the leader's attention those things which are keeping the organization from meeting its objectives. Problems are what an executive's life is all about. If she is going to help, she needs to hear about them. How often have you heard a church committee chairperson or field director exclaim, "Well, I didn't even know he was having a problem"? She may have had all the information needed; the person who sent the information may have believed that all the facts were obvious. Unless the one reporting indicates that there *is* a problem, many times the executive will not analyze it as such. There's an old saying in management that goes, "If the manager doesn't know about it, it hasn't happened," and that's the way most managers have to act. Your responsibility is to *tell* your manager what you need.

The Third Thing

. . . your manager needs to know is *what you are planning to do in the next reporting period*. Plans can be changed. History cannot. That's why plans are like statements of faith. They are our prayerful statement of what we believe should happen.

Your description of your plans indicates:
1. The direction in which you are headed.
2. The fact that you know a direction.
3. Your commitment against your objectives.

"Can two walk together, except they be agreed?" (Amos 3:3 KJV). Since by definition plans are things that lie in the future, your statement of where you're going gives your manager, and your fellow workers, an opportunity to put in objections, opinions, or corrections.

The Last Thing

. . . an executive needs to know is what happened, past activities. He/she *needs* to know about activities and progress, but history is only a report. There is nothing he/she can do to change it, but at the same time it is an indication of direction and an explanation of plans suggested and problems encountered.

Useful Reporting

We suggest that you submit a regular written report. It may be needed once a week or once a month. You and your superior can decide that. But have one.

Recognize here that the *writing* of the report may be even more valuable than the reading. A written report demonstrates that the *writer* has thought the problem through. If the writer asks the questions: "What decisions do I want my superior to make? What problems am I facing? What are my immediate plans?"—all in light of "What has happened?"—a great deal will have been accomplished.

We further suggest that you divide your report by *major objectives,* usually a program or project. Avoid dividing it by *activities.* It's not very helpful when reporting on the progress of a building to indicate how many beams were cut or how many square feet of concrete was laid. What we're interested in is whether the framing was done and whether the foundation is in.

The difference between objectives and activities is not always clearly understood. Objectives or goals are things to be accomplished. They can be stated in the past tense: "Letters requesting the information have been sent out to twenty-two people involved." Activities are the processes through which we reach objectives. "We are writing to twenty-two different people." Objectives, or goals, are therefore directly related to specific times. Activities tend to be timeless.[1]

If all you do every day is activities and never achieve a goal or an objective, either you and/or your organization is in trouble. If you don't know what your (measurable and accomplishable) goals are, either find out what your boss thinks they are, or establish your own and share them with him or her.

It is certainly acceptable to have additional reporting categories such as "general" or "administration" or "miscellaneous" in a report, but these should come last.

Against each of these projects or programs, you should report *decisions* needed by your superior, *problems* you are facing, *plans* for the next reporting period, and *progress* during the last reporting period.

Reverse the Order in the Report

Although the most important item is the decision needed, we suggest you reverse the order when actually reporting: 1) Progress, 2) Plans, 3) Problems, 4) Decisions. Reading a report in this order helps the executive understand the need for the decision.

Highlight each item heading by underlining it. If you have no problems or require no decisions, omit the item. Your omission will indicate that you had nothing to report.

Using Reporting Dynamically

Reports that give only past history are dead, static kinds of things. One reads them and files them away. Reports that forecast plans and request assistance or decision are alive and dynamic.

Use them as the basis of face-to-face discussions. If you have not had such a reporting system before, where possible it is a good idea to schedule regular meetings to review not only content, but the extent of detail in the report. This will help both the supervisor and those supervised to discover both the kinds of decisions the supervisor wants to reserve for himself or herself and those that should normally be made at a lower level. It will give

---

[1] If you need help in this area, may we suggest a delightful book by Robert Mager, *Goal Analysis,* published by Fearon, Belmont, California, 1972. Ed Dayton has also covered this in *God's Purpose/Man's Plans,* MARC, 1974.

the person reporting a feel for how much and what the supervisor wants and needs to know.

As the supervisor is faced with decisions pending (ones asked for in a previous report), it becomes obvious if the program is being hampered *by the supervisor.*

Reports As Cross-Communication

Wherever possible, individuals reporting to the same person should share copies of each other's reports. This not only keeps everyone abreast of what is going on but gives insight into different management styles and approaches.

Sharing your report to your superior with your subordinates keeps them on top of what's happening. If you have things to share which should be in writing, but should not be made public, put them in another memo.

Reports As History

When it will be useful in the future to have an historical record of a program or project, this type of Decision-Problem-Plan-Progress report can be exceptionally valuable. It gives insight into the type of difficulties faced and how they were resolved. By calling attention to decisions needed in one reporting period and then noting decisions made under "progress," the report gives an inside view of the project.

If it is normal procedure to report a number of different projects or programs in the same report, care should be taken to use the same nomenclature each time. We suggest that different projects be delineated with a headline and, if necessary, some project number be assigned.

The Importance of Goals

By now it must be abundantly clear to the reader that we believe that goals are fundamental to any organization. Regular reporting of the type we are advocating is of minimum value if the organization and the individuals do not establish measurable and accomplishable goals with a significant number of checkpoints (milestones) from the beginning to the end of the project. Suppose a local church places someone in charge of "evangelism." Unless it goes on to define what it means by evangelism, who is to be evangelized and when, the reports later issued about evangelism may be

AGENDA

For_____

On_____

Time	Item	Decision	Problem (discussion)	Plan	Progress

Figure 1

nothing more than one person or committee's report of what they think is happening. They will tend to center on activities.

Reports of Meetings

Notice how nicely the Decision-Problem-Plan-Progress format fits into the reports of meetings such as those of a church board. Where the board reserves its decisions to itself, the minutes can indicate that a decision is pending for the next meeting.

In setting up an agenda for meeting, the Decision-Problem-Plan-Progress categories can be used as headings against each agenda item. Place the agenda items to the left-hand side of the page and then leave four columns for "Decision-Problem-Plan-Progress" on the right. If a decision is to be made at this particular meeting, indicate that fact with an "X" under "Decision." If discussion is needed to overcome problems being faced, indicate that with an "X" under "Problem." If you are asking people to do some future planning, place an "X" under Plan. If the agenda item is only to report progress, note this with an "X" under "Progress." Figure 1 illustrates what we mean.

Obviously, any agenda item might include all four of these.

Good Communication

Good communication is the lifeblood of an organization. The more complex the organization becomes, the more attention needs to be paid to an effective communication system. If each person within the organization attempts to discover what the leader wants to know and communicates on the basis of that understanding, organizational effectiveness can be greatly enhanced.

The Special Case of Number Two

There is a great deal we have yet to learn about the function, structure, and operation of not-for-profit organizations. Peter Drucker has noted that most of our management experience comes from the world of business, and we cannot necessarily extrapolate what we have learned in this sector to the other sectors of government and not-for-profit organizations. We have already pointed out (Chapter 1) that the local church may be the most sophisticated organizational concept in the world. The local church has the seemingly impossible task of ministering to the world while at the same time welcoming in any volunteer who chooses to be a member, *regardless of his/her qualifications for service.* (Try *that* one sometime in a profit-making business.)

Should There Be a Number Two?

We introduce this idea of the difference and complexity of the Christian organization because it may well be that the Christian organization has a special need for the one-on-one organizational structure in which there is a chief executive officer (CEO) with one person reporting directly to him or her—a "Number Two," the special situation in which two people are charged with the management of the organization with the ultimate authority lying in the hands of one.

There are probably historical reasons for this arrangement. Many Christian organizations are brought into being by an individual with a pioneering spirit and a great burden of service. The burden may be to start a new church, launch out in a new ministry, or find a better way.

Since most Christian organizations operate on the basis of donated financial support, the original leader often finds himself or herself filling the role of fund raiser, minister, manager, and all-around entrepreneur. As the ministry expands, the need for additional help is apparent. In the local church, this is the time when the congregation talks about getting an "assistant for the pastor." In the service organization, the board may begin to point out to the chief executive that he or she "needs help." The result is usually a Number Two. Who this person is and how he/she performs is often the key to the success or failure of the organization.

Why one person? Why not three or four or five people who each has a special responsibility? There is no one answer. But it seems to be in the nature of things that few individuals have all the gifts needed to lead all the functions of a growing organization. And even if they do, there is just not enough energy nor enough hours in the day to do this effectively. At the same time there may not be the resources (or the need) at the moment to bring in a large staff of people. And, perhaps just as importantly, there is little in the experience of the typical entrepreneurial leader that makes it easy to "manage" a group of people. There seems to be a need for a special relationship with one competent person who can be almost an alter ego to the top executive without necessarily having a dual *final* authority. (Some organizations have attempted a shared leadership, but there is little hard data to indicate that this is an effective procedure.) The Christian organization which (one hopes) is modeled on the concept of a bodylike relationship, can particularly benefit from this arrangement.

Some Examples

We have already mentioned the assistant pastor. A better example might be when an experienced person is brought in as Number Two. Here it is assumed that because of experience, the Number Two has as much to give as to learn. In other words, he or she is not an apprentice.

Many organizations have a Mr. (or Ms.) Inside and a Mr. Outside. Usually the CEO is the Mr. Outside with his or her opposite number "running things" in the office. In this case the Number Two person usually is strong in management while the CEO is strong in the ministry function.

Some organizations (including businesses) have an Office of the President shared by two or more persons. There is still one person with ultimate authority, but they operate like a team and try to present to the outside world a united and integrated front through the idea of an "Office."

The Importance of Number Two

How easy it is to put all the importance on "Number One"! The phrase has almost become synonymous with "Look out for me!" And yet how different from the biblical concept. Perhaps one day we will be able to really understand what it means to be the *body* of Christ in the manner of Paul's first letter to the Corinthian church. Too often we give lip service to the idea of serving one another. Seldom do we see that this may be the most effective management idea conceivable. For *God's* work to be done there need to be godly men and women. Some of those will have vision, insight, and a cause to lead. Others will be needed to bring the vision into reality. An organization of any size may fail or succeed on the basis of its CEO. But it is important to see that the same organization may also succeed or fail because of the capabilities of people like an effective Number Two.

Who *will* be the greatest in the kingdom?

How to Be a Good Number Two

The best place to start is with the concept of *making a success out of your boss*. At first glance this may seem like putting the individual before the good of the cause. On the other hand, if you believe that God has brought the CEO to this task, then there is nothing more important than making the CEO successful.

Understand the CEO's style. Leadership styles will vary. It's likely that the Number Two will be the more managerial person. Analyze where your different styles can complement one another.

Emphasize loyalty. If the Number Two is actually on a one-over-one situation where all the rest of the members of the organization report to him or her, then it is easy to believe that he or she is the one in charge. It must not be seen this way. The organization must always understand the views of the CEO. There must never be any doubt in the minds of the staff that the Number Two has anything but the good of the CEO in view in his or her actions.

Often the CEO will have a clear idea of where the organization should go but will need a Number Two to enunciate this philosophy and to communicate it to the rest of the organization. Learn the CEO's views and *find ways to communicate those views*.

The Number Two person will usually be the one responsible for carrying out the *mechanics* of the planning function. Make sure that *adequate planning time* is spent between the CEO and the Number Two. See that special times are set aside for preplanning discussions.

There should be no surprises. In the beginning of such a relationship there often will be, but both individuals need to work at reducing the number. The Number Two must understand the limits of his or her authority and must, if necessary, spell those out in writing so that the CEO can understand what the Number Two believes are those limits.

How to Be a Good Number One

It takes time. Often the CEO will be so relieved by the idea that he or she has found a competent Number Two that he/she will drop most of the management problems into the Number Two's lap with a sigh of relief. But just as the Number Two needs to learn about the CEO, so must the CEO work to learn the skills and limitations of the Number Two. There is *mutual learning going on here*.

The CEO needs to be open to change. A strong Number Two will undoubtedly have suggestions for running the organization more effectively. Many times this will be threatening to the CEO. Both sides need to remember that the basic reason why the Number Two person is there is to bring about change, to make the organization more effective than it has been in the past.

Channels of communication need to be kept open. One way to do this is to share one another's "reading file," copies of all correspondence to everyone. In this way the Number Two person can begin to understand how the CEO thinks, and the CEO can learn a great deal about how the Number Two may be managing the organization. This kind of relationship takes constant work. Nothing takes the place of openness and a policy of "no secrets."

Conflict should be expected. Strong individuals will differ. Iron sharpens iron.

Number Two May Not Become Number One

We are all familiar with the principle that we should be grooming our replacement. Interestingly, at the top of an organization this is less likely to be true. For many of the reasons mentioned above, the kind of person who is most effective at being Number Two in a Christian organization may not be the most effective CEO. Most often there should not be in either person's mind or heart the idea that the Number Two is being groomed for the Number One spot. Debilitating for both, it can be threatening for the CEO and it can be disappointing to the Number Two.

Who Is Qualified for Number Two?

Perhaps we shouldn't be surprised to discover that it is often more difficult to find an effective Number Two than it is to find a Number One. There are, of course, the very human reasons for wanting to run one's own organization. It is difficult to sublimate one's goals to another.

The ideal person is one who has demonstrated already that he/she is capable of running an organization on his/her own. For example, in a large church the most effective Number Two may be a person who has been the senior pastor of a smaller church. Even better would be someone who has been in charge of a *larger* organization, for what the growing organization needs most is someone who has already operated in an organization of the size that this one hopes to become (see Chapter 19, "A Matter of Size").

Another way of saying the same thing is that an effective Number Two is someone who has already been "successful." In other words, such people no longer have the tremendous *need* to succeed, to prove themselves.

Often the most acceptable person is one who enjoys knowing that he/she has been responsible for desirable change without necessarily needing the outward trappings of authority and power. This person brings the kind of self-confidence so useful when trying to be both a good counselor to one's superior and to interpret his or her purposes and goals to a staff.

Perhaps no other attribute is more important than spiritual maturity and wisdom. The person up front needs wise counsel from someone whose ultimate loyalty is at the feet of Jesus. Every Paul needs a Barnabas. If that person can be in the same organization, it is a special blessing.

For Further Reading

Organization by Ernest Dale covers all aspects of organization: line and staff, general staff, the chief executive and his staff, reorganization, international operations, and the impact of computers on organization. Many organization charts are included. Hardcover.

11   You
and
Your Wife

JIM SMITH IS thirty-eight years old. He has a pretty wife, two beau-
tiful children, and is considered one of the outstanding pastors in
his city. Jim and Jane were married while Jim was still in seminary.
Their first child was born during his senior year. Jane never completed her college education but took a job to help Jim through
seminary. Jim is an effective preacher and is greatly respected by
both his assistant pastor and the congregation. He works hard on
his sermons. His church is growing.

Jim's wife will leave him next week.

Bob Ramson is the executive director of Christian Commitment Abroad, which he founded twenty-two years ago. He has
traveled all over the world and is a much sought-after speaker.
After a shaky start, CCA began to grow rapidly about ten years
ago. Much of its growth is due to Bob's high level of commitment
and his willingness to give himself unstintingly to the work of
Christ.

Bob doesn't know it, but he left his wife and children eight years
ago.

Where Are You?

Where are *you* as a Christian leader? Where does your commitment lie? Could it be that you too are one of those, perhaps without even knowing it, who has left his wife?

How do you sort it all out? Where do your Christian priorities lie? How does one find a balance between commitment to the task and commitment to one's family?

Three Priorities

In our book, *Strategy for Living,* we laid out what we consider to be three levels of Christian commitment, three levels of priority. Simply stated they are:

First—Commitment to God in Christ
Second—Commitment to the body of Christ
Third—Commitment to the work of Christ

We picture these as foundation stones, one built upon another. We begin with the initial commitment to God through his Son. But the visible evidence of this vertical relationship with God is found in this second priority of horizontal relationships with the sons and daughters of God. The Bible calls us away from a Western individualism back to a biblical corporate unity. It is on this foundation and within the framework of this bodylike relationship that the work of Christ is to be carried out. "It was he who 'gave gifts to mankind' . . . He did this to prepare all God's people for the work of Christian service, in order to build up the body of Christ" (Eph. 4: 11, 12, TEV).

These priorities cannot be exclusive of one another. All three are needed. One of the *conditions* for effectively carrying out the *work* of Christ is the relationship that exists within this body. "If you have love for one another, then everyone will know that you are my disciples" (John 13: 35, TEV).

Where Is Your Wife?

We are addressing ourselves here as Christian leaders, and especially as married men. What we are saying here applies equally to a working wife, but since that is a minority situation, we'll deal with it as though we were speaking only to husbands.

Where does your wife fit in your priorities? Certainly of all the relationships described in the Bible, the highest and most mystical is the relationship found in marriage. Paul could only compare it to the relationship of Christ and his church (Eph. 5: 21–33). The disruption of this relationship can have tremendous spiritual consequences. Peter tells us that interruption of the relationship can even interfere with our prayers (1 Peter 3: 7).

Is your ministry as a Christian leader built upon a foundation of a strong marriage relationship, or does it move forward in spite of that relationship?

What about Your Calling?

Some of us immediately respond in our own defense, "But this is the ministry to which God has *called* me! My wife understands that. That's one of the sacrifices that we are making together." Perhaps. But perhaps that is *your* view of the situation, and although it may be outwardly shared by your wife, perhaps inwardly (consciously or unconsciously) she feels quite differently.

Too often the Christian wife is put in the position of appearing to oppose the will of the Lord if she does not feel at ease with the circumstances within which her husband is moving. Many men and women marry before they have a clear picture of the ministry to which they (or he) may be called. Too often they overlook what the Spirit may be saying to *her* and what gifts God may have bestowed upon her.

It's an Uphill Battle

The wife of a dynamic pastor or Christian leader is in an uphill battle for survival as a person. Many times she has sacrificed herself and her own education only to see her husband educated right out of her intellectual life. The public affirmation that comes to him, the sense of accomplishment that he feels in pursuing his career, can only be shared by her in a secondhand way.

Consider the number of opportunities you have for social interaction as compared to your wife who may be home caring for children. Consider the tremendous difference and variety in the type of work that you do as compared to hers. Is it really possible for her to enter vicariously into all your feelings of success?

Of course, there are many husband/wife teams who really *are* teams. They truly have had a common call to the work in which the husband may be employed. They see themselves as sharing a joint ministry. We know some pastors whose wives have a real part in helping them with the planning of their sermons and who play a real role of leadership in the local church. But for many, this is far from the case. And as the initial intensive occupation with raising a family and "becoming established" is exchanged for the changing realities of mid-life, many wives of executives (Christian and otherwise) begin to wonder whether this is all there is to living. Many conclude that it is not.

In her book *Passages,* Gail Sheehy gives us another dimension of the problem. Adults, like children, go through different crises (passages) in life. "Life begins at forty" is true in different ways for men and women. Often it signals a divergence of common interests which can put severe strains upon a marriage if the reasons for them are not understood.

How Do You Stand?

Here's a little test for you to take:
( ) I usually take work home at night.
( ) I haven't had a date with my wife in two weeks.
( ) I don't have a date with my wife listed in my appointment book.
( ) I usually work away from home more than ten hours each day.
( ) We have had two fights in the last two weeks.
( ) We haven't had a fight in five years.
( ) I have four or more years education beyond my wife.
( ) We married before I was called to my present task.
( ) Our youngest child is 16 to 20.
( ) My wife hasn't been on a trip with me in four years.
( ) Most of our social relationships revolve around my work.
( ) The family dinner is often interrupted by phone calls for me.
( ) My wife has little understanding of how my organization works.
( ) My wife has had no additional formal education since we were married.
( ) My wife does not have any career plans outside of our marriage.

If you answered yes to most of these questions, perhaps you've already left your wife or are in the process of leaving her.

What Can You Do about It?

Begin by asking yourself, "What does this mean?" to each of your answers above. This question may suggest to you some steps which you could take immediately.

Start asking your wife for dates, just you two together. Use them to explore how she feels about what she's doing and what you're doing. For example, share your appointment books and calendars together. What do you jointly think about the way you're spending your time? Who have you been with? Who are your friends?

Ask her to evaluate how she sees *you* spending your time. What does she picture you doing? For each item does she feel it's too much, too little, just right? Don't be surprised if your wife first tells you that everything you're doing is just fine. After all, to live with this situation for this many years it has been necessary for her to justify what you're doing in her eyes.

Make separate lists of your individual and joint commitments, commitments to things like work, children, friends, the bank, church, whatever. Sit down and compare your lists. Are you committed to different or similar things? Why do you have differences of commitment? Are they "normal," or do they indicate to you a different understanding about what your common life is all about?

Try to fantasize what you believe would be the very best situation for you as individuals and as a couple ten years from now. Where would you want to be living, what would you like to be doing, what would your relationships be? What are your wife's gifts? What is *her* calling? Where do her gifts and calling fit into the picture for the future? Together set some long-range goals for your life together and for your individual development. Decide on some immediate steps to meet these goals.

If your wife has never had a career, what kind of career would she like? How could she go about being trained for this? Both of you may reply that a career for her at this time in your life is impossible. But what about five years from now? Ten years from now?

You know your wife as well as anyone else, probably. If you were a counselor to her and she was seeking a job, where would you recommend she look? What do you think she might be most equipped to do?

Without opening up the whole question of completely shared responsibilities at home or the growing idea that couples should alternate in their work, are there not some things you might learn to do for her? One pastor's wife we know recounts the story that early in their married life when they had very small children, her husband used to spend an hour each morning following her around the house and reading out loud from either a religious periodical or a newspaper. In this way she learned where his attention was being focused and thus they could spend some profitable time together.

Consciously reschedule your life by leaving blocks of time available, unscheduled. Use these to give yourselves more time together, to be more able to respond to each other's needs. Most of us can't instantly change our lifestyle, but we can plan to become free of some future responsibilities.

Prayerfully consider whether you really do believe that the priorities we have suggested above are biblical and operative in your life. God's work *will* get done without you. God is really not nervous about the future. Isn't he much more concerned with what you *are* than what you accomplish, and isn't what you are demonstrated by the relationships you have? And isn't the most profound of those relationships the one you have with your wife?

Have you left your wife?

We pray she will take you back.

For Further Reading

In *Strategy for Living* we have tried to suggest some ways in which you might work toward corporate goals for your life. *Strategy for Living* has an accompanying workbook that you and your wife could work through together.

In *Tools for Time Management* by Ed Dayton there is some useful information on both the concepts and the practice that we have suggested above. Our pastor and his wife, Ray and Anne Ortlund, have looked at part of the problem in *The Second Half of Life*.

12 You
and
Your Board

ALMOST EVERY ORGANIZATION has, or should have, a board of directors. For no matter how competent the leaders of a Christian organization or a local church may be, there is always the need for a "disinterested party" who can stand back from day-to-day operations and exercise wisdom and judgment on behalf of the organization and its leadership. God does his work through men and women!

When Do You Need a Board?

There is a tendency to believe that only growing or larger organizations need a board. Just the opposite is the case. The small, struggling organization desperately needs the kind of assistance a good board of directors can bring to it.

Types of Boards

There are a number of different kinds of boards, and all have their role. A *board of reference* may be made up of men and women whose names will authenticate the work of an organization. Normally they have no other function than to be aware of the organization's overall purposes and goals.

A *board of advisors* is usually made up of people competent in the same field as the organization. With no legal responsibilities for the organization, they serve because of their interest in the general purposes of it. They give mostly technical assistance.

The board we wish to discuss here is a *board of directors,* a group of men and women who have legal responsibility for the organization.

The Purpose of the Board of Directors

The board of directors serves three general functions: first, it serves as a board of review. Second, it serves to install or remove top management. Third, it serves a function in public and community relations. For the Christian organization there is a fourth dimension, that of spiritual leadership.

In its *review function* the board should help set policy to insure that the organization is carrying out its objectives, to make certain that the organization has developed strategies, that it is doing long-range planning, that it is handling its investments well, and that it is maintaining a good *esprit de corps.* In many ways the board is just someone that the management can talk to. Normally a board of directors will carry out its review functions by being actively involved in a number of committees, such as finance, audit, and personnel. The latter generally reviews the salaries of top leadership executives.

The board of directors has an important role in the *installation* and *removal* of *organizational executive leadership.* This is probably the most difficult function the board has to perform, yet the most important. For a failure of leadership will almost always result in the failure of the organization.

The third major function of the board is that of *public* and *community relations.* The board can carry out many tasks that the executive members of the organization might find it difficult to do. It can supply contacts for the organization and help to establish working relationships with other groups.

The role of *spiritual leadership* is very difficult to define. Perhaps the only way to express it is: find Spirit-filled men and women through whom God can operate.

Selecting the Board

For a board to play its role and carry out the functions we have described above, it needs to be carefully selected. There are a number of questions to ask as we go about this process:

How large should a board be? Probably the smaller the better. The size should be determined by the number of people available to constitute a quorum, the frequency of board meetings, the amount of representation of different constituencies that is needed and the amount of work the board will have to do to carry out its function. Perhaps for most Christian organizations, from five to fifteen is a good rule of thumb.

Who should be selected to serve on the board? Certainly go for the best men and women you can find. This is particularly important when originally constituting a board. Start at the top. The willingness of new members to serve on the board will be greatly influenced by the caliber of the people who are already board members. This speaks strongly to the need to search for, cultivate, and eventually attract community and Christian leaders. On the other hand, we do well to avoid Christian "celebrities." People who are very prominent in their own right may bring a constituency with them, but remember, they will take some of it away when they leave! Board members make an impact when they join the organization—and they make an impact when they leave!

Look for enthusiasm and a desire to serve, balanced by an ability to make a good contribution. The people you want will usually be committed to other important activities. They will need to be convinced that they *can* make a contribution to your organization and that what your organization is doing is important. Once they are convinced they will normally be enthusiastic.

What should be their spiritual qualifications? We need men and women of spiritual maturity. This does not necessarily mean mature in years, though normally the two will go hand-in-hand. We need men and women who are well-spoken-of by others, people who have demonstrated an ability to manage their own Christian affairs. Find ways to observe and evaluate as much as possible in this area. Remember, we are not only concerned with whether people are able to express themselves in godly terms. We want to see how such godliness has been worked out in the day-to-day business of living and carrying out the work of an organization.

Should they be insiders or outsiders? In other words, should the board include members of the paid staff? Most American organizations vote yes. But make sure that the balance is maintained. A ratio of one insider for two outsiders is perhaps a good suggestion.[1]

---

[1] Some consumer "watchdog" organizations believe that there should be no more than one paid staff member on a board. For the Christian organization this appears unduly restrictive.

What kind of a mix of different people should be on a board?
Think about what kind of a mixture of ages, sexes, professions, experience, Christian background, connections, and prestige you would like to have. Perhaps you need to give consideration to ethnic representation. However, avoid tokenism. Too often women or minority groups are brought on a board not because of what they contribute but only because of the people they represent. Make sure that they, too, have gifts to provide and roles to play.

As you think about the different people for the board, think about how they will work together. You're not always looking for agreement, rather you want a balance of viewpoints. Make a chart with the kinds of people you want listed down one side and the types of jobs or roles you want them to fulfill on the board across the top. Try to analyze what kind of person would best fit each role.

Who should choose the board members? In the case of the self-perpetuating board, obviously the board members will be elected by the existing board. In the case of a local church, the ecclesiastical tradition and the practices of the church will be followed. However, for the nonchurch Christian organization, many times the recommendation of the management will be carefully considered. Often the top management or leadership will propose board members and do the research necessary to bring them up for nomination. Consequently, the chief operating officer of any organization does well to cultivate and maintain a background list of people whom he or she feels would be outstanding members of the board. Many times it is a good practice to select the board of directors from an advisory board. Indeed, some organizations make this mandatory.

To keep the board vital, you might want to consider a rotation system, with a prescribed time off the board before reelection.

Board Operation

Committee work within a board is important. It expedites the work and keeps members involved. Be sure areas of committee assignment fit the experience and interest of the individual members.

Accurate corporate minutes are vital. Be certain to have a capable secretary or at least staff assistance for the secretary if needed. After all, the minutes of the board meeting are essentially the formation of corporate policy.

A strong chairman is needed, not to be the decisionmaker or the one to exert undue pressure, but one who would guide the board meeting carefully, secure input from all participants, note the sense of the meeting, and seek to head toward consensus. The chairman is the key to a successful and harmoniously functioning board.

Preparation for board meetings should be done well in advance. An agenda should be prepared and background reading should be provided. Recommendations that will be made by the leadership to the board should be spelled out as much as possible in advance. If the board is to develop confidence in management, then the management must do its homework. Since good board members are likely to be busy in other activities, meetings of the board should be planned at least three meetings ahead even if this stretches out two years in advance. In this way board members can budget their time accordingly.

Supporting the Board

Orient and educate new board members to how the organization operates. Each organization has a special jargon of its own. Provide them with as much background information on the organization as possible without overwhelming them with too much material. If there is a house organ, make sure they read this. Send them a policy manual if you have one and the minutes of previous board meetings as well. Shortly before the first meeting which they are to attend, contact them personally either by phone or mail, welcoming them to their position and explaining in detail how their first board meeting will operate and what their role in it will be.

It is the executive's responsibility to keep board members well informed regarding the organization's activities. The board should not only read such material carefully, but respond with suggestions and encouragements. An uninformed or poorly informed board member can cause unnecessary problems and difficulty in a board session. This requires a constant and very specific flow of information between meetings.

It is the responsibility of the executive to keep in close touch with the board and to provide them with everything they will need to function wisely. Don't overlook the need for board members to get to know one another. Provide opportunities for socializing and mutual support. Many local churches have a practice of taking the board on a weekend retreat as part of the first meeting after election of new members. Organizations which may only have quarterly or semiyearly meetings need to think of similar ways of bringing relationships closer.

Don't overlook the *cost of supporting a board.* Consider it as a well-warranted expense. Usually your board members will be giving you their time at no cost. However, you may need a policy which covers some or all of their travel expenses. It may be advisable to spend money on the setting in which the board meets. These are problems which need to be discussed within the board, but it is the role of the executive to bring them to the board's attention.

One of the most effective things an executive can do to support a board is to make sure it continues to work on the organization's long-range plans. After all, it is only as the board has a clear understanding of where the organization has been, where it is now, and where it intends to go, that it is able to give wise judgment. Good planning is the context within which good decisions are made.

Whether it be the pastor or the chief executive officer of the Christian organization, each needs to take a personal interest in the board members. Seek out opportunities to have a luncheon date with them. If they live in different cities, make sure they are contacted if you have occasion to be in that city. As you see that they have special skills, contact them for personal advice. At the same time, let them know that you are open and available to help them if they see occasions where your knowledge and experience can be useful to them.

How to Avoid the Rubber Stamp Board

This is a question we have been asked a number of times. Many Christian leaders feel frustrated because instead of giving policy guidance, their boards seem content to go along with whatever leadership suggests. What can be done? This process cannot be accomplished overnight. It may take as many as three to five years before you can develop the kind of a board really needed to make the organization function effectively. But by setting out a description of the kind of a board you need and then working to fill openings that come, you can have a sense of moving toward your objective and eventual success.

If you are in the process of forming a new board or expanding a present board, then the suggestions above should move you a long way toward avoiding a "rubber stamp" board. On the other hand, if you already have a board that is giving you inadequate input or direction, there are a number of things you can do: first, analyze the skills and capabilities of the present board. Second, try to define specific job descriptions for members of the board. Third, consider a rotation system or an expansion system which will permit you to bring new blood onto the board. These three moves will many times encourage present members who are really not willing to become involved to gracefully move off the board.

The board of directors has a tremendous impact on the potential of any organization. The time and energy invested in clearly defining roles, carefully selecting members, and supporting the members once they are selected, will produce long-lasting dividends.

For Further Reading

See Ernest Dale's *Organization,* mentioned earlier.

13 | You and Women Leaders

WITH ALL THE TALK about "the Christian woman" and the attention devoted to recognizing that men *and women* have been created in the image of God, it is surprising how little has been said about what it means to be a Christian woman at work in the world. Little has been written about the role of women in Christian organizations, let alone the role of women as Christian leaders. When we first wrote on this subject in an issue of the *Christian Leadership Letter* we were startled by both the positive and negative response to our comments. It is evidently a hot subject in many quarters. But the fact remains that regardless of what those of some Christian persuasion might believe (i.e., whether it is even biblical for a woman to work outside the home), thousands of women have moved beyond this position. We need to speak about their role. What we will say here will be mostly addressed to men, since it is a fact of life that men still dominate the ranks of Christian leadership.

Women in History

Christian organizations probably have more women in roles of leadership than almost any other type of organization. Both the Old and New Testaments are replete with women leaders. Deborah led the people of Israel. Priscilla and Lydia were Christian businesswomen. Euodia and Syntyche were noted by Paul because "they have worked hard with me to spread the gospel" (Phil. 4: 3, Good News Bible). Women missionaries have been outstanding in their zeal and in their leadership. In 1976 there were approximately 4,650 North American *single* women missionaries. They have preached, planted churches, administered programs and done practically everything their male counterparts have done. As an aside, one wonders why some Western churches have had so much trouble in accepting women in roles of leadership when they have been exercising all of these gifts overseas!

While many denominations are coming to the conclusion that women should be ordained, some denominations have had women pastors for many years. In 1977, 17 percent of seminarians were women. Many Christian organizations are led by women. They include denominational executives, as well as women in positions of leadership at all levels.

Are Women Second-Class Citizens in the Kingdom?

Our answer would be a unequivocable no! But so as not to confuse what follows, we will not enter into the discussion of "headship" and especially the role of men and women in marriage. Although the Bible has always pointed to women as having a significant role in the affairs of the world, we still find within Christian organizations a good deal of male chauvinism that is cultural rather than biblical.

It would take an entire volume for us to work through all the biblical data that leads to the position which we assume. Rather than do that we point you to the book by Don Williams, *The Apostle Paul and Women in the Church,* which we believe does an excellent job of analyzing the various positions, all of the pertinent biblical data, and sees the Bible as not only permitting but sanctioning in some cases the leadership of women over men as the situation warrants.

Men have traditionally been cast in the mold of the protector, leader, hunter, and sportsman. Perhaps the reason men seem to have fared better in the business world and the world of organizations is that business is a competitive field. We men have been trained from the time we were very little boys to be competitive. We have been taught to *win* at sports, to fight for each rung on the ladder of success, to compete for the hand of the woman we love.

In contrast, our culture teaches women not to fight (in that sense of the word). Often it seems they have been taught to be passive rather than aggressive. Somehow the passive qualities have been associated with being feminine, and since women are conditioned to be feminine, they hesitate to exhibit aggressive qualities. This passive role is emphasized over and over by the media. Movies, television, and reading materials have only recently begun to portray women moving aggressively toward well set goals. Usually women have been portrayed at home, dressed in a frilly apron, cooking for the family, or as the sweet innocent waiting for her hero to come and rescue her from peril.

Transition from Past to Present

Women are trying hard to overcome these images that have so long been a part of our cultural heritage. It's an uphill battle. Those who have been educated side-by-side with men through twelve to eighteen years of school are faced with a society that says woman's natural future is to fall in love, marry, and stay at home to raise a family.

Change always comes slowly. It is frustrating to try to change a tradition.

The Cultural Perspective

For Christian men and women who have lived all of their lives in one culture, it is difficult to determine how much their own culture has conditioned their view of the Bible. When we hear that perhaps over 50 percent of the leaders of African churches are women, there's a natural tendency to wonder if they really have interpreted the Bible correctly. It is difficult for some young women to become independent of the life style their parents would have them follow. It is difficult for some parents to let go of a dream they have had for their daughter if she chooses to do something other than follow the cultural pattern.

A good case could be made for the argument that the reason single women missionaries outnumber single men is that this is the one role in which women are allowed to exercise all of their God-given gifts. The reduction that has been noted in the number of single women missionaries in recent years would seem to bear out this thesis.

Those of us who used to smile at attempts to eliminate sexist language are slowly beginning to see how conforming such language can be. We are also saying that it is not impossible, as it seemed at first try, to eliminate such language.

In spite of our rightful and historic concern for the home, over 50 percent of married women in the United States are working.

It is also a fact that on a job-for-job basis these women receive significantly less remuneration for their efforts. Meanwhile, married women who also work must be outstandingly good managers. They are essentially asked to handle two jobs at the same time.

Are Women Different?

You had better believe it! But wait a minute. Let's remember that to some degree we are *all* different. Among men we find those who are passive and those who are aggressive, those who are introspective and those who are outgoing, those who are task oriented and those who are oriented toward relationships. It is probably safe to say that the *spectrum of difference* among working men is much broader than the general difference between men and women in working situations.

The Christian Organization's Attitude toward Women

It is not difficult to trace why many Christian organizations are heavily weighted with women in low paying clerical positions. First, the routine repetitive type of operation is one that requires a minimum investment on the part of the organization. Unskilled housewives or housewives-to-be are natural candidates.

Second, many women come to work to help the family over a financial hardship while the husband is in school or just beginning his career. Too often these women take jobs considerably below their educational experience.

Third, since many (most?) Christian executives have not had formal management training, they don't value the training a number of Christian women are receiving in schools of business.

Fourth, we are children of our culture. We (naturally) see the Bible through the lens of our own culture. One of the things that our brothers and sisters from churches in other lands with other cultures are helping us to see is this very fact. Until one has moved as a Christian among the churches in many different cultures, none of us is even aware that the Bible might be read in a way differently than we see it.

Should We Change?

We think so, both for the good of the organization and in recognition of the contribution that women can make. Jesus acted toward women in ways that often defied the culture of his day.

It would seem strange that his church should have to learn the lesson of woman's equality from the culture!

What Are Your Real Feelings?

As we said earlier, this chapter is directed primarily to men who, since they hold the majority of leadership positions, are the ones who are going to have to make a major change in their attitudes. What are your feelings about women in executive positions?

— Do you see any biblical reason why women can or should not play executive roles?

— Are you personally threatened by competent women? Why?

— Do you believe that women are not capable of learning the same managerial skills as men?

— Does your organization have significant numbers of women with college degrees doing semiclerical work?

— Do you have a significant number of women on the staff who have been with the organization for a number of years without receiving increased responsibility?

— If you are the pastor of a local church, do you give the same titles to men and women on the paid staff?

What You Can Do

If you believe the Bible clearly states that women should not have leadership over men, then there is not much more to say. We respect your interpretation of God's Word, but as brothers in Christ we ask that you consider ours. Too often we have a tendency to read one another out of the kingdom over matters that are not essential to the heart of the gospel.

But assuming that you want to take a hard look at the role of women in your organization, what can you do?

— Look at your current staff. Are there women there now who have the latent gifts and primary education to qualify them for more responsibility if they were men?

— What steps would you have to take to give them more responsibility and commensurate authority? What career paths might you imagine for them?

— Since in many organizations it is still a man's world, any woman you do help along is going to have to prove herself. Are there women on the staff now whom you consider outstanding? (In our management seminars we often discover the

person who scores the highest on the supervisory skills test is a woman.)
— What additional training would be necessary?
— How can you use training, responsibility, and promotion to model for the organization that women have a leadership role to play in God's economy?
— Take a look at your written procedures, memos, and policies. Are they heavy on sexist language?
— Write to the best Christian schools of which you are aware. Ask them to recommend to you women who appear to have special abilities. Seminaries are graduating more and more women.

Problems

It is one thing to believe that women can and should be used more effectively in the leadership of Christian organizations; it is quite another to put them to work.

There is still a great deal of conscious, and even more subconscious feeling on the part of most of us men about women leading. A female member of our executive staff once commented, "When a man gets promoted he says to himself, 'I deserve that!' When a woman executive is promoted she tends to say to herself, 'How lucky I am.'" It's no easy thing for a woman to work in a man's world. On top of this, the woman executive is often put in charge of other women who, for some of the reasons we mentioned earlier, do not understand that in her executive role she must operate in quite a different way. For the male leader it's difficult not to be "one of the boys." It is doubly difficult for the female leader not to be "one of the girls."

Women *are* different! It is normal for both men and women to respond differently to someone of the opposite sex. This needs to be faced, honored, and handled carefully.

Because women are the bearers of children, their decision to get married can have a profound impact on any future organizational career. (On the other hand, this is often a smoke screen we put up. Take a look at the average time a male member of your staff stays with the organization.)

Where Now?

Women need the encouragement and support of men (and other women) to become all that God would have them to be.

They need to be accepted as equal business associates and as individuals who can think knowledgeably and perform effectively. Given the opportunity, there are many women who would surprise themselves, as well as their fellow workers, at how well they might carry out an executive position.

For Further Reading

We were very impressed by the writings of Catherine Booth. Her small booklet, *Female Ministry,* was first published in *1859!* What surprised us was how well she covered almost all of the biblical data now being discussed. You can get a copy of the booklet by addressing the Salvation Army, 1314 West Ninth, Los Angeles, California 90813. The cost is 95¢.

Earlier we referred to the book by Don Williams, *The Apostle Paul and Women in the Church.* Williams first discusses the various popular positions on women, both Christian and secular. Second, he analyzes all Paul's statements about women verse by verse. He then draws conclusions with which we generally agree.

Part III

You
and the
Organization

14 Planning As a Process

IT IS APPROPRIATE that we open this section with a discussion on planning. We have covered the details of how to plan in some of our other writing.[1] At the end of this chapter we will suggest many resources that will be helpful to you.

The important thing is not *how* you plan, but *do* you plan?

Why Some Organizations Don't Plan

Perhaps if we first discuss why some organizations don't plan, this will help you to see where your organization fits. This apparent lack of concern for planning can be explained by a number of factors:

— Most Christian organizations are fairly unsophisticated in terms of forecasting their "income." Thus, they tend to think of the future only in terms of expendable dollars, funds they have on hand. Some organizations even make this a matter of practice. They view spending all the money as it comes in as exerting greater faith and trust in God. Consequently, if asked whether they have plans for new things for next year, they have no detailed answer.

— The dynamics of Christian service are such that many of those involved consider it impossible to think more than twelve to fourteen months ahead. Who knows how God will lead? And

[1] See our book *The Art of Management for Christian Leaders,* and Ed Dayton's workbook *God's Purpose/Man's Plans,*

yet many Christian organizations are continually making decisions that will have tremendous impact on their future. For instance, for the local church, the decision to build a building has repercussions that will last for years ahead. The decision of a foreign mission agency to enter a country commits them to supporting such an endeavor for many years.

— There is still a question in the minds of many as to whether planning is not attempting to invade the sphere of the Holy Spirit. After all, no one can predict the future, and planning seems much like an attempt to do just that.

— Not only are the financial resources of many Christian organizations limited, but so are the human resources. There is a natural tendency to believe that any thinking about the future must be done in the context of people who will be available.

What Are the Facts?

It may not take much thinking to recognize that none of these factors are really valid:

— What next year's income *may* be can be ascertained from what the past three years' income has been, with some correction for the general economic situation. What next year's income *can* be may be analyzed on the basis of the per capita giving of the constituency, what similar organizations are receiving, and what other ways there are of displaying the need. But all of these concerns aside, the first question is not "can we?" but "should we?" The question of money should always come after the question of need and goals. If we therefore first make our plans and then correct them on the basis of what we think our income can be, we will at least know the direction in which we are moving.

— Likewise, human resources are limited only by our ability to motivate people through our goals. You don't often motivate people directly. Rather you find people who are already motivated toward the type of thing you want to accomplish.

— It is true that the Lord may change directions for us, but that is *his* business. Ours is to make statements of faith (goals and plans) around and toward which we can work. Christians act out their lives in faith between the unresolvable paradox of God's sovereignty and man's complete responsibility.

— James sums up the question as to whether we should plan or not: "Instead you ought to say, '*If the Lord wills*, we shall live and we shall do this or that' " (James 4:15).

We Should Always Be Planning

Management has often been characterized as a series of major phases, sometimes three, sometimes four, sometimes five: planning/acting/evaluating; planning/organizing/operating/ controlling; organizing/planning/leading/controlling/evaluating. Although this process is usually depicted as a closed, repetitive circle, there is a tendency to think of these as steps: we plan; we act; we evaluate; we replan.

Such thinking can be dangerous for the not-for-profit organization and especially for an organization that uses volunteers. Why? It assumes that if one group plans adequately, then another group will act accordingly. Sometimes that group will. But not very often. If we give the planning function to one group and the "working" function to another group, we will greatly diminish effectiveness because people like to work against their *own* plans.

Planning As a Process

We need to see that planning is a process, a continuous process. It begins before the "acting," but then continues alongside it. It is helpful to think of planning as acting, evaluating, and replanning—including problem-solving. We have tried to indicate how this cycle works in the figure on page 131.

Put Planning to Work

Christian organizations have a singular advantage over secular organizations in that they can anticipate, and plan for, a high degree of goal ownership. Such goal ownership is obtained by *participation in the planning process*.

What many organizations do not realize is that planning can be a very useful way of involving many people in considerable depth. The act of asking individuals or groups to consider alternate or optimum ways of reaching their goal, or the act of asking them to propose specific goals against the higher purpose of the organization, can be the trigger for a series of events. It cannot only give people a feeling of having participated in the organization, but it can stimulate a host of new ideas. This is just as true for the local church as it is for the Christian organization which uses no volunteers.

Horses and Camels

In any discussion about the future, bringing in as many people as possible early in the process will produce a greater possibility of anticipating and handling objections, as well as gathering bright, new ideas that you might otherwise miss.

Many people think that a camel is a horse designed by a committee. One reason is that they weren't on the committee!

Planning in Itself Brings Change

Sociologists have recognized for a long time that the very taking of a survey can change the situation the survey was attempting to uncover.

To illustrate the impact planning can have on a group, consider the change that can be brought about by a simple questionnaire. To draw an extreme example, suppose a questionnaire was circulated within a congregation with two simple questions:

```
1. Do you believe that our church is
      (  ) moving ahead?
      (  ) standing still?
      (  ) falling behind?

2. Do you believe that our pastor should be
      (  ) replaced?
      (  ) retained?
```

However ludicrous the second question might appear, it is obvious that the very fact of its being asked will raise all kinds of questions in people's minds.

To give an example of a failure to bring about change, how often have you seen a church "planning committee" spend months on a plan only to have it rejected? Most such committees violate the cardinal principle of planning groups, namely, that the function of the planning group is to find ways of implementing the goals of the parent organization, not to generate such goals themselves.

Why Planning as a Process?

What does all this have to say about the use of planning as a process within a Christian organization?

First, we need to be continually asking everyone concerned for their dreams about the future. Where do you think we should be in five years? What is your vision for what our organization (church) can be or do ten years from now? As you look around you, what needs do you see that our organization should be meeting?

This has many benefits: it keeps reminding everyone that there *will* be a future, and they need to be prepared for it. It gives them an opportunity to reflect on what kind of future is most desirable and where they might fit into it. It communicates the idea that leadership is attempting to lead by exploring as many future avenues as possible.

Second, have a regular planning cycle that is short enough to be practical. For most Christian organizations in Western countries this will be a yearly cycle. But don't compress all the "planning" at the end of the year. If a planning system is to work, hopes and goals for the future need to be spelled out well in advance of any approval date. For example, if the local church is working on a yearly cycle that requires approval of next year's budget in late November, then certainly that church needs to start its planning cycle in early spring. Too often we start our planning and budgeting at the same time. Don't fall into the trap of planning by "extrapolation of the budget"! In this method, each item of the budget is considered against how much was spent last year and an estimate made of what increase or decrease will be made for the coming year. The total is then added and if it exceeds what the organization believes it can expect to receive in terms of finances, the whole budget is reduced. This is fatal to creative thinking. Plans first, money second.

Third, have a separate long-range planning system within which the yearly system operates. For most Christian organizations, three to five years is as far ahead as it is practical to make any concrete plans. But unless we think well past the present planning year, there will be a great tendency to be overly concerned with what we visualize *can* be rather than what we believe *ought* to be.

Always ask people to do their next year's budget within the context of the last two years and the coming two years. When you ask people to set goals for next year, also ask them to set goals for two and three years from now. We recognize that a good percentage of the goals we set two and three years ahead will have to be modified or replaced. The point is that we lay better plans for the future and make better decisions about the present if we make them in light of some picture of how we think the future will be. We need to see such long-range planning as an arrow that points direction rather than a given set of steps to be followed.

Fourth, have a planning function, committee, staff, or at least an individual, whose task is to *help others* through the planning process, to train people in how to plan, to integrate the plans of the total organization by pointing out gaps, overlaps, conflicts, and the need for further definition.

One of the major functions of this committee should be to *keep the future visible.* This means we have to plan for planning by scheduling the events of the planning cycle well in advance and encouraging everyone concerned to see these as important events.

Fifth, involve as many people as possible in the process. In a local church, this will normally mean having a yearly "planning conference" in which anyone who wants to can come and share his or her dreams and hear reports and discussion about where we've been, where we are, and where we hope the Lord is going to take us. This, of course, cannot actually be a *detailed* planning conference in which the final plan is worked out. Rather it should be seen as a major step in the *process.* We think this is so important that we have devoted the next chapter to the subject.

Sixth, recognize the invisible hand of the informal group. The volunteer organization needs to be particularly sensitive to this. There are always groups of people who have the interest of the organization very much at heart, but who (at this time) may not be in formal positions of leadership. Do your best to understand where these people are and to solicit and listen to their ideas. Who some of these people might be we discussed earlier in Chapters 2 and 5.

Seventh, remember that effective planning is incomplete planning. Don't *over*-plan. It tends to inhibit people's creativity and eliminate a sense of participation; it fails to take into account that things will change. Rather, we should see that the very open-endedness of plans will keep people alert to the fact that they have to be continually planning. Planning *is* a process. This means that we should be careful not to plan beyond our ability. By this we mean that if your organization is new to planning, don't try to cover everything. Gain experience as you go along. To be a detailed planner you have to first learn to be a general planner.

Last, remember that good planning does not always succeed. We can go further and state that planning *should not* always succeed. Good planning accepts risks; and therefore some are doomed to fail. If an organization has a 100 percent batting average in accomplishing many programs, you can be fairly sure it took no risks or chances.

Using Planning As a Tool

In a day in which history is accumulating at a rate which almost threatens to engulf us, our only reasonable defense is an attempt to anticipate what tomorrow may be like and how we will respond to the opportunities and challenges it presents. By making planning a process with the organization, we give ourselves one tool to undertake such a task.

For Further Reading

Parish Planning by Lyle E. Schaller is subtitled "How to Get Things Done in Your Church." It not only contains its own good bibliography, but it is an excellent basic source book. Paperback.

The Human Side of Planning by David W. Ewing is one of the few books on planning that deals with all the obstacles to making good planning work for you. It lays out in honest detail the type of human interaction needed to implement any plan. Hardcover.

Group Processes: An Introduction to Group Dynamics is Joseph Luft's introduction to group dynamics. A good book for someone who wants to gain a more technical understanding of group process, including such concepts as the Johari Window, interaction patterns, metacommunications, as well as group process and organizational behavior. Hardcover and paperback.

15 Holding a Planning Conference

HAVING DISCUSSED THE NEED for planning and having seen planning as a process in the previous chapter, we turn now to one vehicle which is particularly appropriate for the Christian organization, and especially the local church—the planning conference.

Probably most Christian executives and pastors agree that planning is an asset to effective leadership. Possibly just as many of us would admit that we do far less planning than we believe we should. The difficulty is that planning *takes time*. And time is a commodity which is in continual short supply. So many things have to be done right now! Who ever heard of a Christian executive or pastor who didn't have too much to do? The enemy of planning is the tyranny of the urgent. Just about the time we sit down together to figure out where we go next, our secretary announces a newly discovered brushfire that demands our immediate attention.

Good planning requires extended periods of quality time, the right mix of people, the right environment, and the right preparation. Or, to put it another way, good planning is the result of good planning.

One of the best ways we know to maintain a continual flow of fruitful planning is the vehicle of the planning conference. By this we mean a conference which is isolated from the interruption of everyday fire fighting, which is purposely constructed to produce the desired result, and which is planned far enough in advance so that all needed participants can be available and be adequately prepared. Let's begin by discussing the last of these, the element of time.

How Often Should You Hold a Planning Conference?

This is another way of asking, "How often should one plan?" This is part of the larger question of how much time we should give to planning. Planning should be a continuous process. When we sit down at the end of the day or early in the morning to scratch out a things-to-do list, we are doing daily planning. When we put an hour aside with members of our staff at the beginning of the week to talk about the week ahead, we are doing weekly planning. Many Christian organizations and local churches find that a monthly planning meeting with the entire professional staff is a good way to keep one's house in order. However, in terms of setting new goals and deciding how we are going to reach them, you will want to consider quarterly, biannual or annual times with the appropriate staff together. The planning conference meets this need.

What Is the Goal?

"The goal of a planning conference is to plan, right?" Wrong. The goal of this kind of planning conference is to discover how to reach goals through plans. Therefore, it may be necessary to include as an early item on the conference agenda a definition of goals—measurable, time-bounded statements of achievements. But by its very nature of having people together for an extended period of time, a planning conference gives potential for doing a number of other things. It can have a number of goals. Not the least of these is *team building*. By now most of us are conscious of the positive benefits that result from shared goals and shared plans. As people work together setting goals, making plans for them, and then working to bring those goals into reality, they learn to appreciate each other's strong points and to work around each other's weaknesses. They have an opportunity to experience each other as people and as individuals.

Another goal of the conference may be *training*. How you set up the conference and how you hold it will say a great deal in itself and will become a model to help others lead their own group's planning. The best way to learn to plan is to be part of an effective planning meeting.

Obviously, the ultimate goal of the planning conference would be *to move* the organization toward its purposes.

What's on the Agenda?

The answer should flow out of the goals you have set for the conference. There will be announced goals and unannounced goals. Some of your unannounced goals would include how you want people to feel as a result of the conference and what modeling or training you want to do.

How you begin will do much to set the climate for the hours that follow. Take into account the total amount of time you have, how far afield you are willing to let people stray in their discussions, what kind of closure you are hoping for, and the "product" you would like to have at the end of the conference.

There is always a tension between activity and prayer. The amount of time spent in consciously drawing the participants together as those who are about God's business will depend upon the history of the group before the conference. But in any case, avoid beginning in such a way as to leave the impression that we are giving a nod to our Lord and then moving about our own business.

If the goals you are working on are only roughly defined, then the *clarifying of goals* needs to come quite early in the agenda. Make sure that the people who come have all the information they need to formulate the goals. This may be information they bring with them, or it may be in the form of presentations made to inform the participants so that all have a common base of information. Copies of such things as annual reports, individual department or staff reports, data about the area in which you are working, resources in the form of specialists or consultants may all be needed. Avoid sending large masses of material to people at one time. If the participants need a great deal of material in order to be prepared, consider sending it out to them on a weekly basis before the conference. This will be helpful in two ways: first, it will not leave people so overwhelmed that they never get around to reading the material. Second, it will keep reminding them over a period of time that they are moving toward this conference.

Schedule time for changes of pace. This may take the form of exercise, just plain relaxing, or going about the same problem in a different way. Remember, for most of us work is really fun! It's only when we have too much of the same thing that we tire quickly.

Consider using two or three people to make a presentation. Just hearing a different voice many times calls us back to attention. Vary the type of audiovisuals that you use (and make sure you use them!). Some things are best presented on an overhead projector, others can be done with charts or on the chalkboard. In selecting audiovisual methods, consider both the idea of change of pace as well as the technical needs of the conference.

Allow time for personal expression. Too often we go to conferences where we are spoken to, and even though there is a time for "response from the floor," many people are never really given an opportunity to express how they are *feeling*. This is why the idea of having "reaction groups," a smaller number to break up and discuss what is presented and make reports back, is so valuable. But also use this reaction group time to allow each person to share his/her feelings at the moment.

For example, one conference in which we were involved went this way: after the reaction group had discussed the matters laid before it, time was left for each member of the group to express how he/she was feeling about the conference, the way things were being conducted, as well as about the material in hand. At the end of this sequence there was a time of prayer within the group. This way it is hoped that each person felt he or she had been heard. The time of prayer not only reminded them as to *why* they were about the business they were, but also gave them opportunity to pray for each other's needs at the moment.

Somewhere on the agenda should be a time of *summarizing* and drawing to a conclusion. We all need to have a sense of closure. Some people have such a great need to produce that if the conference ends without their believing that anything has issued forth from it, they will go away needlessly discouraged. Make sure that when you leave everyone understands his or her responsibilities and assignments. Just the fact that we know there are certain people who are going to do things after this conference is over gives the whole conference a sense of conclusion and perpetuity.

If you are going to use a planning system which is new to some of your staff, such as PERT, bar charts, flow diagrams or graphs, make sure that you give *adequate training* in their use (see the suggested readings at the end of the previous chapter for more information on planning tools). This is a good opportunity to do some team building by having people work on sample planning problems and then try to analyze some of the difficulties of the system. This helps to separate the process from the content.

How Long Should a Planning Conference Last?

Probably at least two days. There is something helpful about having the planning time divided by a good night's sleep. Taking two days, with the evening in between, is a natural way of using the first day to gather and present data and the second day to go to work on the data and convert it into goals and plans. "Sleeping on it" is a great way of synthesizing many ideas, calming tempers, giving time for second thoughts, and just plain letting ideas sink into our subconscious. And you just can't rush it.

On the other hand, if the situation in your organization or your local church is such that it is not practical to be away overnight, then try to imagine ways that might be functionally equivalent to this. For instance, you might want to schedule the formal business of the planning conference from 9:00 in the morning until 3:00 in the afternoon and then schedule two and one-half hours of participation type games, a long hike, or perhaps the showing of films or the presentation of a drama that has nothing to do with the *content* of the planning conference, but which might have a great deal to do with the Christian life.

Unless you have some people who are skilled in the hard work of planning, anything beyond two days is likely to produce ever-decreasing results. Planning is hard work. It takes a great deal of attention and concentration.

Where Should You Hold a Conference?

Try to find a place sufficiently isolated from your office so that it will be "impossible" for you to be interrupted. It should be far enough away that it will be difficult for people to return to the office, but not so far away that it will require too much travel time. Perhaps there is a resort an hour's drive away. Perhaps there is another church or organization willing to lend you its facilities.

Make sure the meeting place is comfortable and that there are facilities for exercise breaks and other forms of relaxation.

Make certain that all of the planning tools you need are available, including easels, projection equipment, photo-reproduction equipment, dictating and transcription equipment (if needed), and anything else you might use in your planning procedures. Prepare a checklist ahead of time and make sure in your negotiations with the facility that you are very clear as to what they will provide and what you will bring.

Many local churches use the facility of another local church. This has the dual advantage of moving away from your environment and also moving into a setting dedicated to the same purpose as yours. Perhaps a tour of this other church's facility, or a presentation by a member of its staff on *their* goals and purposes, might make a real contribution to your conference.

Similarly, Christian organizations can exchange sites. Often there will be a Christian college nearby which will have the facilities you need.

Who Should Come?

This can be an extremely sensitive question. It is even more difficult if you are going to take a number of staff people physically out of the office. Their absence is going to be noticed, and others will draw their own conclusions as to why different people were invited. If at all possible, you should announce your reasons for taking the people that you do. Obviously you can work faster with a smaller number of people, but usually the longer way around will be the shorter way home. The more people who are part of the planning, the more likelihood there is that you will get good acceptance of the plans when an attempt is made to convert them to actual practice. (To quote Peter Drucker, "Eventually all plans must degenerate into work!")

You may want to differentiate between those who are going as the planning team and those who are resource people. There may be specialists who come in to make presentations or to act as advisors but not to do the planning. Another type of person whom you may want to consider is the "facilitator" or "enabler." This person should have skills in group dynamics and perhaps has had experience in putting on planning conferences. He/she cannot only help in the actual carrying out of the conference, but can help you in the planning. Sometimes there's a great advantage in having someone from outside the group. This person will appear to be more neutral, and the instructions he/she gives as part of the presentation will be accepted more readily.

If your conference is being held within the context of a local church, obviously there will be certain people who will come as a result of their position on various boards or councils of the church. But consider inviting the entire congregation as participants. You can make a reasonable assessment as to how many people will respond to your invitation (and whether you can financially afford to have them!).

But regardless of whom you eventually decide should be included, make sure that the ground rules are well established so that you avoid embarrassment later on.

Do a Good Job!

If you want to model good planning, do a good job of planning your planning conference!

Lay out a schedule of events to take place prior to the conference: people to be notified, material to be gathered, prior work to be accomplished. Build a checklist of things to do: facilities checkout, equipment list, visual aids, training aids, transportation arrangements, meals and so forth. A good way to make sure that everything is covered is to write the instructions for what needs to be done on the back of a postcard and then mail it to the individual responsible a week before he/she needs to begin. This brings us to the next most important thing.

Put someone in charge of the project of holding the conference. The person need not necessarily be the leader. This can be a good training time for the younger manager. Be certain that this person doesn't think the whole burden rests on him/her. Coach him/her in delegating. As new need is uncovered, the first question should be, "Who could do the best job of this?"

Understand the communication media you are going to use. There is a difference between a *process* and *content*. Content has to do with the message you want to deliver. Process has to do with making sure that the content is received in the manner in which you intended. How people feel about the planning process, how they communicate with each other, how they receive the acceptance of their ideas will all have a direct bearing on an ultimate goal which is usually expressed as content. So do your best to imagine how those taking part in the conference will "hear" what is being said and in what setting and under what circumstances they feel most comfortable about making their contribution.

Review and rehearse. If you are going to take ten people away for two days, you are utilizing a good many work hours. This is a big investment. Get it down right before you begin. This could include reviewing with a number of people the amount of time you have allocated for each segment of the conference, making certain by direct contact with them that everyone who is going to make an input understands what he/she is doing. Often a "scenario" of the entire conference is very useful: across the top of the long side of an 8½ by 11 sheet of paper make columns for Time, Event, Person in Charge, Materials Needed, and Anticipated Outcome. By then filling in these columns for each time segment and distributing the scenario to everyone involved, all of the leadership of the conference will have a good understanding of where they are in the process and how they fit.

Evaluate as you proceed and when you have finished. Usually an evaluation meeting halfway along will help the conference leaders discover where conference goals are or are not being met. And if you are going to do better next time (and you should), you had better find out what were the strong points and the weak points of this conference.

The Planning Conference As an Event

Some organizations, especially local churches, have discovered that the planning conference can be used as an all-organization event. The idea is to gather ideas from as many people as possible with an eye toward having each person feel a part of the total process and then share in the goals and plans which may result. At first this may seem like an undertaking which could lead to nothing but chaos. If, indeed, chaos is to be avoided, then such a conference will have to be well planned and well managed. Those doing the planning must have a good understanding of where the participants are and what process they must go through to reach useful conclusions.

The key to such conferences is to spend a good deal of time gathering data and sharing ideas. Here is where many of the books and papers on brainstorming and group process can be used to good effect. By dividing the large group into smaller subgroups and by having the subgroups brainstorm around similar or different topics, a way can be found to have each individual make a contribution. This needs to be more than just an exercise. Plan on ways of gathering information from the groups, synthesizing it, and then putting the groups back to work on higher priority items. Usually the best results are obtained if the group process is used to sort through perceived needs and desired goals. These needs and goals can then be prioritized and may in themselves become an overall statement against which detailed plans can be made.

Many times such conferences, particularly where volunteer organizations like local churches are involved, can be done as a two-step process. The first session is used to gather ideas, while the second session is used to put groups to work in doing specific planning. In this case it is helpful to pretrain group leaders, particularly in planning techniques.

Where Is God in All of This?

As Christians, we have a great advantage over those involved in other endeavors. We believe that we are participating in God's strategy for the world! Make certain that you remember this and through the spoken and unspoken words of the conference keep reminding all of the participants.

For Further Reading

A large book useful to anyone planning an extensive conference is *Achieving Objectives in Meetings* by Richard Cavalier.

Joining Together: Group Theory and Group Skills by David W. Johnson and Frank P. Johnson is a great resource book. It will help you with many of the group dynamic situations you will want to include as part of a planning conference.

16   Assumptions

THERE IS A NATURAL CYCLE to healthy organizational development which begins with *purposes,* moves on to *goals,* imagines
ways of meeting those goals with *plans,* and then *acts* on those
plans. Life being what it is, *actions* need to be continually *modified*
against plans, and most *plans* need *to be changed* as we go along.
Finally, as the process is about to begin again with new goals and
perhaps refined purposes, we hopefully *reevaluate* our purposes,
goals, plans and actions against the lessons of our history. It's a
circle:

This simple picture is a way of telling ourselves what we have to do. It's also useful in telling each other where we are. If we don't understand the cycle, or we fail to communicate, we are much less likely to be effective.

But there is another failure of communication that can do us in—failure to *state our assumptions*. At each step in the cycle we need to consciously consider and tell one another what we believe about the world in which we are working, our mission, ourselves, and the future.

Failure here can lead to some severe breakdowns in communication ("Oh, I didn't know you were assuming *that!*"), and ultimately a failure to achieve our goals.

Christian organizations are particularly susceptible to this failure, for we consider so many of our assumptions to be facts. After all, we have a world view that assumes a God who not only created the universe, but who is active in history. We see ourselves as attempting to be conformed to his good will for us. Aren't these all the assumptions we need?

We think not. Furthermore, we think there are some simple steps to be taken by any organization that can open up the whole area of assumptions and thus uncover potential misunderstandings.

Assumptions Present and Future

The assumptions we are concerned with are grouped primarily around the present and the future, rather than the past. What do we assume about the world in which we live? What do we assume about ourselves, our capabilities, our theology, our ministry? And what do we assume about this same world ten years from now, about ourselves and our ministry ten years from now? Do we have the same assumptions? How much do they differ? We will suggest some ways you can use to help people not only state their own assumptions, but also hear what others are saying.

When to State Assumptions?

There is no best time, but probably the occasion of redoing our goals, or reviewing our purposes, is a good time.

But the question, "What are we assuming here?" is always valid. Too seldom in the midst of our problem solving do we stop to ask one another, "What assumptions are we making at this point?"

How Do We Go about It?

We have supplied a beginning list of questions that may be helpful (they begin on page 135). We would suggest that somewhere in the goal-setting and planning process all of the major participants be asked to individually list their assumptions under a given set of categories. Don't try to be too precise in the questions. Let people state their assumptions as they feel them. What you are after here is an expression of the milieu in which people are thinking. For example, your request might be, "To have as broad an understanding as possible, we would like each of you to write down, in any order, your assumptions about the world, our organization, our purpose, anything at all that you think important to understand as we carry out our mission."

You may want to do this anonymously, allowing each participant to submit an individual list.

Once this has been done, one or two people should compile a new list under some headings which appear to make sense for your situation. For example, you might want to group assumptions under such headings as Fund Raising, Administration, and Ministry. Or, you might want to group them under headings such as World Situation, Christian Situation, and Our Situation.

Once these have been compiled they should be resubmitted to the group so that everyone can see the others' assumptions. At this point there are two things which you need to evaluate.

1. Is this assumption important to us in our ministry?
2. Is the assumption valid?

One way of going about this is first to categorize the assumptions and then set up two major columns after each written assumption on an 8½ by 11 inch piece of paper. Entitle the first column "Important to Us?" Entitle the second column "Probability or Validity." In each one of these columns you can ask each person to rate his/her reaction to the assumption under the typical five categories of Strongly Agree/Agree/Neither Agree nor Disagree/Disagree/Strongly Disagree. Obviously there is no sense worrying about an assumption that everyone agrees is probably true, but few people think is important to the organization.

Again, the results can be compiled showing how many people in the group had a common view and how many had a diverging view. Where there is a degree of disagreement, an open discussion is perhaps in order.

What to Do with the Assumptions

Let us assume that you have followed the procedure above and you now have a list of assumptions which the majority of the group agree are both important to your ministry and probably are valid. What now?

Go back and review your purposes and goals in light of these assumptions. Which of the goals or purposes are impacted by them? Which of your purposes or goals seem less realistic or more realistic in light of these assumptions? Which of these assumptions bear on your future planning? If you have already done your planning, do any of these assumptions change your planning? Is there a need for a new goal or a new plan?

These goals and assumptions should be made a part of the long-range planning of the organization.

Assumptions As a Scenario

Another way of getting at assumptions is to try to write "future history" by means of a scenario of coming events. Since your goals should be timebound and dated, what will have to happen in order for them to be realized? Put yourself a few years into the future and then look backward. Try writing a news story in the same way a news reporter would write it. What happened? What events took place both within your ministry and within the world in which your ministry operates? *Why* did these things happen? The "why" will show you some things you may not have known you were assuming, things you couldn't plan for but on which you were counting.

Review Your Assumptions

There ought to be a regular time at which last year's planning and goals are reviewed for both success and failure, as well as lessons learned. This is also the time to review your assumptions. Which ones turned out to be valid? Which ones turned out to be of no importance? What does it tell you about your assumptions for the next planning cycle?

Good for Big Tasks and Little Tasks

You will discover that this assumption-writing exercise is helpful not only for large and complicated tasks, but also for small ones. You will also find that when people are going through the problem-solving process, it is a helpful communication exercise.

Some Suggested Questions about Assumptions

How long will there be a continuing need for our ministry? How do those who are benefited by our ministry feel about it? How will they continue to feel?

What factors may come about which will change our ministry?

Will the world situation within which our ministry operates continue as it is, or will it become less stable or more stable? How will it become more or less stable?

Will there be a growing acceptance of our ministry?

What are we assuming about the people through whom the ministry will be carried out?

What type of people will we need for the future? Will they be available? What will be their needs?

What are we assuming about the stability of our own organization? Will it continue to have the same leadership five years from now? What might cause a change in this?

Do we expect our organization to grow in size? Finances? Breadth of ministry?

What will be the availability of finances?

What will be the impact of inflation?

What other economic factors are likely to take place that will have an impact on our ministry?

What are our theological assumptions? What are we assuming about the spiritual life of our people?

What do we expect to happen to other organizations who are in a ministry similar to ours?

Will the present organizational structure still be viable and in place five or ten years from now? If not, how will it differ? What will cause it to differ?

What portion of our ministry will no longer be useful in ten years?

Why do we assume this is the best way? Is there a better way?

For Further Reading

Values and Faith by Roland S. Larson and Doris E. Larson is a happy wedding of value clarification exercises with an exploration of the Christian faith. It is a good source of group procedures and educational approaches that will fit many applications, including clarifying values in family, church, and community settings.

17 | Where Does the Money Come From?

ONE OF THE MOST PROMINENT but least discussed problems in every Christian organization is, "Where does the money come from?" Money does peculiar things to our thinking. If our church or other Christian organization has a significant bank balance, someone may say, "My, the Lord is really blessing!" On the other hand, if it is in short supply, we may hear, "Too bad; they are really suffering for the Lord!" Or worse yet, "I guess that really wasn't the Lord's will for them."

Money *is* a very personal thing. If you don't believe it, the next time you are in a social group, ask someone how much money he/she earns each year and listen for the deathly silence in the rest of the room!

But we need to *talk* (and write) about money. For money is one of the great "tools" that God has given us to carry out his business.

Input—Process—Output

Let's try to fit money into a proper perspective. Every organization can be thought of as going through a three-step, repetitive process of (1) *inputting* resources into the organization, (2) *processing* those resources in order to (3) produce some form of result or *output*. A manufacturing organization will take money, manpower, and raw material as *input,* and *process* all of this to produce some product (*output*). A service organization will gather funds (*input*) and spend (*process*) these funds in such a way that it will produce a desired service (*output*). A local church will gather together the lives, prayers, time, skills, and money of its congregation (*input*) in an attempt to combine (*process*) these in such a way that men and women are brought into the kingdom of God or that members of the church are built up (*output*).

Thus, we see that it is possible to divide any organization into three major functions: (1) *input*, (2) *process*, and (3) *output*. At World Vision we think of these as being fund raising, operations, and ministry.

Start with the Output

We commented earlier that too many organizations begin with "input"—the funds that they think they can raise. This is the wrong place to begin. Start with the output question: "What is it that God wants us to accomplish?" "Output" can be thought of as objectives, goals, or outcomes that you want to produce. Regardless of how you describe it, this is a place to begin. We need to set high objectives, clear goals—objectives and goals that will make us stretch. These are our statements of faith, our response to what we believe God wants us to do. To think God's thoughts after him, we need to think boldly.

After we have decided what it is that God wants done through us, we should move to the question of the means (process). This will bring us to means and methods—ways of doing things—to which the planning process we described earlier will lead us.

Only after we have looked at outcomes and the means should we turn our attention to resources (input) that will be needed.

Pay Attention to Money

However, just because money is the last thing we should consider in the planning process, it does not mean it should not have considerable attention. If our simple model of input-process-output is descriptive of what we are all about, then we need to pay attention to the input. We need to *set some goals for funding*, to lay plans for funding, to assign responsibilities for funding, and to evaluate our fund-raising performance.

Fund-Raising Goals

Fund-raising goals should be based on ministry goals and not vice versa. Nevertheless, fund-raising goals need to be specific and challenging.

It is true that there are some fund-raising strategies dependent only upon the amount of money raised. A good example is the local church that raises funds for missions against the goal of "50 per cent of the total church budget." But, in general, goals of this type have little ability to stir people's imaginations. They easily lead us to supporting the organization rather than supporting the purpose of the organization. Few people are interested in giving to support an organization, no matter how well oiled it may become. People are interested in what's going to be different. They are interested in the *output,* the results of their investment. Can good stewardship demand otherwise?

One of the reasons so many fund-raising programs fall short is that the projects and programs for which they are intended are not clearly defined. This can be particularly true in the local church which, as the years go by and one pastor replaces another, has a great tendency to see itself as an ongoing establishment rather than a tool in the hands of God.

The reason people are usually willing to give to a building program is that in their mind's eye they can imagine a new building. They can even fantasize that they personally paid for one window or part of a wall. But it is rather difficult to fantasize what part of the average pastor's day a church member pays for.

Anything that can be done to redesign the organizational budget so that it focuses on what is to be accomplished (output) will be a great help in setting and achieving fund-raising goals.

Don't Forget to Plan

A good fund-raising program is not the product of three Tuesday night meetings over the course of a month. Usually fund-raising programs continue to improve because of *evidence of past performance.* If the last time the people gave to your program really thrilled them with the results, chances are they will be ready to give a second time.

If you are a local church working on a yearly fund-raising program, then working a year ahead is none too soon. In the same way that you should continually project a three-to-five-year growth plan or plan of accomplishment, so you should also plan a three-to-five-year program of fund-raising. One is always built on the other.

Resources for Resources

It takes resources to gather resources. It takes money to raise money. This is nothing to be ashamed of. Quite the contrary. We need to make sure that we have allocated *enough* resources.

If we hired someone to do a five-hour job and they took ten hours to do it, we would be displeased. We would think that they were inefficient. The same is true of fund-raising. If we planned to spend $10 to raise $100 and we ended up spending $20, we should be unhappy with our performance. But what happens all too often is that instead of spending $10 to raise $100, we spend $1 or $2 and end up only raising $10. You can do your own arithmetic here to figure out *that* is not good stewardship.

Local churches often miss this point, particularly in their missions program. In an effort to "save money" they produce amateurish looking promotional materials, poor audiovisuals, and the resulting impression is that missions is a second-class business.

But How Much?

How much should you spend for fund-raising? An accepted rule of thumb is that fund-raising costs for charities ought not to be over 20 percent. Notice that we say *fund-raising* monies. We are talking about the *input*. The cost of administering these funds is something else again (we've called that "process").

A local church might think the 20 percent figure very high. This is because so many volunteer hours are available. However, it has been our experience that the budgets for most local church stewardship committees are woefully small. The goals for which they are raising funds may be very good, but if they are unable to communicate those goals, the response is likely to be less than desired.

Is There Enough Money?

We've already said that as we plan we should start with goals or outcomes, then move to means and only lastly deal with resources. Some will immediately reply, "Well, we can't spend money we don't have!" They remember what a tough time they had last year, and they can't imagine that things are going to be better. "You can't get blood out of a turnip."

O ye of little faith! The Bible has as much to say about money as almost any other subject. Do we *really* believe that God is limited in his resources or that God's people are so overextended that there is no possibility of them giving any more to his work?

Perhaps no group has exercised as little faith in fund raising as some "faith" missions. An enterprise that began many years ago to send missionaries has since developed into an extremely complex business of supporting overseas programs. Although missionary support levels have been rising, it is still a fact that in most cases the program cost is one-to-two times that of the cost of salaries and individual support.

We applaud those mission agencies who have put the entire program cost in front of their constituencies. The extent of those costs can be startling. We know of one mission agency working in Colombia, South America, with a team of nine different missionaries where the average program cost per missionary family amounts to over $20,000. To churches who are used to supporting missionaries to the extent of $500 to $600 per month, this may seem like a huge sum. Yet, in reality, this is the amount of money that has been spent.

Too often mission agencies have initially presented to the local church only the individual missionary support costs and then had to return time and time again for additional items such as vehicles, buildings, or the work of a national evangelist.

It is our opinion that the average churchman will welcome an overview of the total cost package and will respond enthusiastically to support those programs with clear, accomplishable goals.

What about Ethics?

There have been a lot of "exposés" about the improper handling of funds in nonprofit organizations, including local churches. Rightfully so. An organization's integrity is perhaps more at stake in fund raising than in any other activity. It is all too easy to spiritualize our goals into such high-flown purposes that we justify sloppy fund raising and even sloppier accounting. All the more reason to get fund-raising costs out into the open. This is one of the reasons we applaud any effort to standardize accounting procedures so that fund-raising costs are separated from administrative costs and what has been lumped together under the euphemism of "overhead" is seen for what it is, namely, the cost of *input* and *process* which produce the ministry (*output*).

May we say a (biased) word here to local churches? We sometimes hear either the staff or membership in the local church state that the local church has no "overhead." (We will discuss the concept of overhead in Chapter 22.) But unless a church spends a major portion of its funds outside of its own precincts, then everything it does is overhead! It is spending all of its funds and resources on itself. There's nothing wrong with this. The church is in the business of people caring for people and winning them to Christ. However, we need to be clear in our terminology.

What about Professional Fund Raisers?

An organization must take responsibility for its fund raising. This is not something which can be delegated away. The use of outside consultants or professional fund-raising organizations certainly has its place, particularly if new ideas are needed. However, choose them with care. Personally talk to other organizations who have had experience using their services. Make certain that your ministry goals are clearly enunciated both to yourself and to those you are going to ask to help you. Remember, you are raising money for a ministry, not for yourself.

Avoid letting professional fund raisers operate on a percentage of the money they have raised. It would seem at first that this is a good incentive, but in the long run it may come back to haunt you. As you think about your agreement with a fund raiser, ask yourself the question, "Will we be welcomed back by our constituency next year if we use this approach?"

Money Is a Tool

It is just a convenient way of transferring resources. Unfortunately, it is often used as a measure for things about which it tells us nothing. Don't be ashamed of your need for money. If there is going to be a ministry (output), then there needs to be resources (input).

For Further Reading

There are a surprising number of books available on the whole area of fund raising. Before purchasing any, we suggest that you look in your local library.

There are some good chapters on this subject in the book, *Marketing for Non-Profit Organizations* by Philip Kotler.

18 Describing the Organization

THIS IS REALLY A CHAPTER about organization charts. Almost every organization has them, but few people understand them. They are variously viewed as showing:

—Authority relationships
—Responsibility relationships
—Personal position or status
—The size of the organization
—Lines of communication
—Importance of different functions
—Paths of promotion

In fact, the organization chart does show all of this information to one degree or another. But what it communicates is greatly dependent on the perspective of the viewer, as well as the designer!

The idea is not new. Moses had a detailed organizational description. He just used a different "language" to describe it!

Regardless of how you go about it, it is very useful to describe an organization. But before going further, let's first look at some "rules" for making organization charts and then briefly discuss their meaning.

Drawings Use "Language"

One of the reasons so many people misinterpret organization charts is that they have not learned the "language." Organization charts fall in the category of what are generally called "logic diagrams." Through a series of symbols they attempt to quickly show relationships. Words are replaced by pictures. The difficulty comes in assigning meaning to the symbols.

Now it should be immediately stated that there are no right or wrong symbols. The important thing is that the symbols have *agreed upon meaning* and that *meaning does not change.* In other words, the organization needs to define for all involved what meaning *it* had assigned. What follows is only *our* definition. Use it as a point of departure for your standard language.

Boxes

A box is used to describe a position or a person or both. (The only reason it is not an oval or a circle is for ease of lettering.) All boxes should be of the *same size and shape* unless they include a number of persons in the same box. In other words, avoid any attempt to relate size to importance. Standard sizes of such boxes are available in label form from stationers and art supply houses.

If you are showing both position and name, it is useful to separate the two with a line in the box:

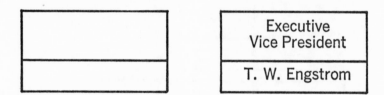

Be consistent in your use of names of individuals. Don't use initials for some and full names for others, titles for some and no titles for others. For example, don't use *Dr.* T. W. Engstrom unless you are going to use *Mr.* E. R. Dayton. Better to omit all titles. By the way, most people are sensitive to the use of all the initials in their name. To use *T. W.* Engstrom but only *E.* Dayton is viewed as demeaning.

Lines

Lines are used to connect boxes and give some "logic" to the organization chart. How lines enter and leave a box is part of the language.

Keep all lines the same thickness. (You can buy thin colored tape to replace inked or pencilled lines.)

Generally lines of authority should enter a box at the top and leave it at the bottom:

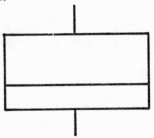

Thus a simple chart with only "line" functions would look like this:

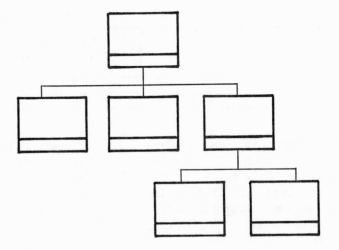

"Line" is another piece of organization language (this time in English). It is usually contrasted with "staff." When we talk of people as being in a line position, we mean that they have people reporting to them and they, in turn, directly report to someone else in such a manner that their unit of responsibility, their suborganization, is directly related to the overall goals and purposes of the organization. In other words, they fall in a line between the production worker and the chief executive officer.

In contrast to this, a "staff" person is usually seen as part of the office of the person to whom he or she reports. We normally give such positions titles like "Assistant to . . ." They are seen as being there to help the position to which they report and its specific activity.

Line people are seen as having stronger positions of authority over others than is true of staff people. This leads us to the addition to this rule—staff positions, individuals whose primary task is to strengthen the individual they report to, or to put it another way, individuals who stand to the side of the top-down line of authority. The best example is the personal secretary or "assistant to" title. But there will be other examples, such as entire staff groups set up to do an investigation and report and/or recommend to someone else.

To differentiate "staff" from "line," the line of authority enters the box from the side:

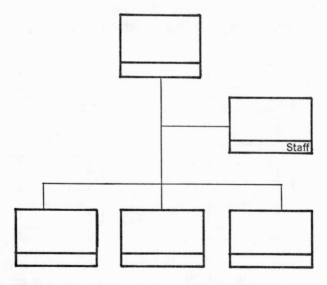

If this position in turn has other positions reporting to it, "line" logic is followed:

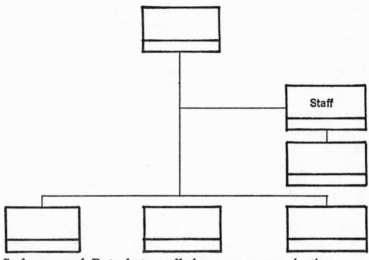

So far so good. But what usually happens as organizations grow and the number of positions multiply, is that we run out of room on the chart.

The temptation at this point is to change the rules in midstream. Avoid it! Organization *charts* tend to grow wider faster than they grow deeper. The solution is to stack equivalent positions on the top of the others in the drawing. In some ways this is good because it tends to minimize the feeling of hierarchies. The way to do it is:

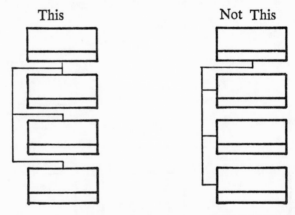

The illustration on the right is wrong because it has the lines coming in sideways to the boxes and thus needs to be interpreted as "staff."

Dashed Lines

You have to decide what they mean. (Be consistent.) Usually they are used to show lines of indirect authority. For example, suppose each of three divisions of an organization has an accounting function, and you want to indicate that financial standards are generated and motivated by the Chief Financial Officer. You might use dashed lines like this:

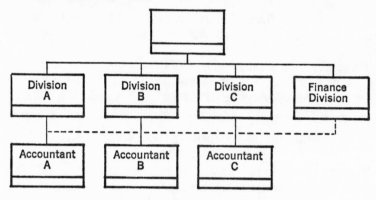

Dashed lines really become important when you have a so-called "matrix" organization. This is an organization made up of both project or group leaders and specialists. The overseas organization of World Vision is a good example. In each geographical region we have a Regional Director. In the same office with each of these Regional Directors is a Director for Development, a Director for Childcare, and a Director for Evangelism and Leadership. But although these three individuals are accountable to the Regional Director for the way they carry out their everyday affairs and how they coordinate with one another, each position reports directly to a Division Head in the International Headquarters. We would show a dotted line from each one of these positions to the Regional Director and a solid line from their positions back to their Division Heads.

However, when one moves down one level we have Field Directors who report directly to the Regional Director and who, in turn, have specialists reporting directly to them. These specialists, however, have a dashed line responsibility very much like the example we gave above of the accountants relating to the Finance Division, to Regional Directors of Development, Childcare, Evangelism, and Research.

Who Should Be Included on the Organizational Chart?

The general rule is to include all leadership functions. If the organization gets so large that it is impractical to show all the functions on one chart, then the usual solution is to have a chart which shows all of the top functions and then individual charts to relate to them.

Remember, the great advantage of the organization chart is that it presents a large amount of information in a small space and in a form available to everyone. If your chart gets too big, you will defeat your purpose.

Individuals Reporting to Committees or Boards

This is a case particularly prevalent in local churches. As a general rule, we prefer using a different shape of block, perhaps twice as wide as the one we have shown here, to indicate the committee. Again, the logic of line and staff should apply. Sometimes, someone is assigned to the committee as a staff person, while at other times he/she will report to the committee. A good example would be the role of the Christian Education Director in a local church. Does this person report to the committee or to the pastor? Obviously, since this person is on the paid staff, there is a relationship to both of these. Here is another application of the dashed line which shows that this individual is related to the committee or to the pastor but reports to only one of them.

Perhaps we need to say a word about dual reporting. If at all possible, avoid it. Practice indicates that it's bad for everyone involved and it takes a very special kind of person to report to two different people. Thus, in the local church it should be very clear whether the Christian Education Director is ultimately responsible to the pastor or to the Christian Education Committee.

Who Should Have a Copy?

At World Vision, we have made the organization chart an integral part of the Employee Manual, a copy of which is given to each employee when he or she joins us.

This is based on our desire to communicate as rapidly and accurately as possible the way we relate to each other and to show the new person where he or she fits.

What's Christian about All This?

Not much. It's a useful tool in your box. Remember, however, that organizations are made up of people who are in *relationship* to one another. Organization charts are one attempt to show those relationships in such a way that the individual relationships will be strengthened and thus the organization will prosper.

What Do They Mean?

So much for the details of construction. What are organization charts supposed to *show*? Some people think that organization charts are supposed to show *lines of communication*. Another view is that organization charts show *lines of responsibility*. A third group might use an organization chart to describe how the organization actually *works*. We would suggest that they be used *only* to show *lines of ultimate authority* and that people be educated to that concept.

There are many reasons for this. First, organizations don't work just the way an organization chart displays them. For example, in the day-to-day business of getting a job done, individuals in different divisions will *communicate* with each other directly. Committees will come and go. Temporary task forces will be formed. Attempts to adequately reflect all of these relationships on one diagram will quickly detract from the primary purpose of the chart.

As organizations grow, the chart helps give management a picture of overall balance and change. It helps people in various positions of leadership to see where they fit in. It also helps the newcomer or outsider gain initial understanding of the relationships that exist and where to enter the structure to get something done.

How Often Should They Be Changed?

Often enough to be useful. If the organization is reasonably stable, perhaps the chart needs to be issued only once a year. If the organization is changing rapidly, every three months may not be too often.

Where to Begin?

If you have been given the task of drawing an organizational chart for an organization that has never had one, we would first suggest that you agree on *your* rules. If you adopt the ones we have given here, fine. In any event, make sure these appear somewhere on the face of the first organization chart you draw so that everyone will understand your "language." If there has never been a chart, you may be surprised at some of the responses you will receive the first time you share one around the organization. If the organization is more than a year or two old, has any significant number of people involved with it, and has never had a chart, it is quite likely there are many assumed relationships. Your first attempt at describing relationships on an organization chart may meet with a good deal of surprise.

For Further Reading

Organization is not a topic that has received a great deal of attention among writers. However, if you want to look at what some other people have suggested, we would again suggest Dale's *Organization.*

A Matter
of
Size

TITLES CAN BE MISLEADING. Appellations such as president, executive director, or pastor give few clues as to what responsibilities are involved. The executive director of Mission A may lead an organization of hundreds of people and be responsible for millions of dollars. The executive director of Mission B may head a group of nineteen people with a budget of $85,000. The pastor of Church C may lead a congregation of 125, while the pastor of Church D may minister to a membership of 2,000.

This same indefiniteness applies to organizations. How large is a "church"? What do we mean by a "foreign mission"? Such names can cover an infinite range of possibilities.

This lack of definition has very real consequences in the failure of Christian leaders to recognize that it requires different men and women with different skills and experience to lead organizations of varying size. In time this failure can bring about organizational atrophy or even demise of a potentially growing organization because the leadership did not recognize that size *does* make a difference. Different size organizations do require different kinds of people.

Not a Matter of Value

Before going further we need to be quick to point out that the ability to manage a larger organization does not necessarily mean greater worth of the individual, be it spiritual or technical. Indeed, there are many men and women heading large organizations who would find it almost impossible to lead a small one. There is not only a quantitative difference; there is, as we shall see, a *qualitative* difference. Each one of us needs to discover our gifts and how and where God would have us use them.

Why Larger Organizations Are Different

At first glance one might conclude that a leader is a leader, and a good manager is a good manager. What difference does organizational size make? After all, if one limits the number of individuals reporting directly to him or her, isn't it about the same? The difficulty with this analysis is people. Organizations are all about people, and people are involved in relationships. To see how this adds to complexity, realize that an organization of 10 individuals has 45 interpersonal relationships, while an organization of 100 people potentially has 4,950! That's just the possible relationships *within* the organization. When we consider the multiplying relationships between the larger organization and its world, the problem is vastly compounded. To cope with this complexity, larger organizations develop extensive procedures, adopt sophisticated tools such as computers, and use a wide variety of specialists such as accountants, analysts, computer operators as well as specialized functions in the form of departments and committees.

Characteristics of Leaders

Let's contrast the type of leadership needed by small and large organizations:

Specialized skill characterizes the leader of the small organization, while the large organization needs as a part of its leadership, a *generalist* whose specialty is management.

The small organization is usually headed by a *doer,* an activist, often an entrepreneur. The large organization more often needs a *planner* or thinker.

Leaders of small organizations tend to be *originators,* promoters of new ideas. They also tend to be *individualists.* Leaders of large organizations have to select ideas from others. They are likely to be *synthesizers* and *team players.*

Small organizations require *supervisory skills.* The leader needs to be close to the everyday work. Often he or she is directly in- volved in the actual doing. Large organizations need *managers* who, while they are always involved with people, are attempting to work through them rather than give step-by-step direction. They need to be *delegators.*

As a consequence, leaders of small organizations are involved with *procedures,* the how of things, while leaders of large organi- zations are concerned with *policy,* the why dimension.

Finally, effective large organizations need leaders with con- siderable education, experience, and skill.

Consequences for the Organization

Let us assume for the moment that your organization has come to the point where you are aware that it is growing and changing. What steps can you take to accommodate to this difference in size?

First, be aware that *leadership needs will change.* Unfortu- nately, few leaders have the ability to grow as rapidly as the or- ganization. The leader must gain new abilities or be undergirded with strong subordinates who are permitted to exercise their skills, or the original leader may have to be replaced.

Second, *plan leadership growth* along with organizational growth. Train, add, and/or replace. This must include time and resources for continued education and interaction with others. This, of course, assumes that someone or some group is respon- sible to be doing this planning. Some organizations place this re- sponsibility in a personnel department. Other organizations have individuals or groups who are specifically given the task of "man- agement development," including the identification of individuals who appear to have potential for greater leadership capacity. Which leads to our next point.

Third, attempt to identify and train potential leaders, men and/ or women who by the time they have matured will be ready and anticipating leading the larger organization.

Fourth, "If you want to know something about a city *ask some- one who has been there.*" If you plan to become a church with 1,000 members, search for a pastor who has led a church of 1,000. If you anticipate your agency having an income of $5 million, find a person who has led an agency of that size or larger.

Larger organizations have faced most of the problems of the smaller organizations and developed standard solutions to them.

People with experience in such organizations don't have to "reinvent the wheel."

Fifth, a reciprocal point to what we have just said, *don't attempt growth beyond the ability of the (entrenched) leadership.* If circumstances are such that present leadership cannot be moved quickly, wait.

Consequences for the Leader

First, *plan to grow.* We mentioned earlier Peter Drucker's speculation that today's average college graduate will have to retrain two times before retirement. The world is changing all too rapidly. As a result, Drucker calls on us to learn to learn, on the assumption that once we have mastered that, all of life can be open to new learning. If you continue as the head of your organization and do not grow, how will it? (See Chapter 4, "You and Your Education.")

Second, *be open to new ideas.* Success is dangerous. Doing it "our way" may mean doing it in a way that will not permit growth of the ministry. Too many people with ten years' experience have one year's experience ten times over.

Third, *bring in people smarter than you.* Identify the needs of the growing organization and find people to meet those needs. You can never be as smart or experienced as everyone working for you. That's all right! Your task as a leader is not to be smart, but to lead people to be effective servants of Christ! We recognize how threatening this suggestion can be. However, it is almost a truism that one of the characteristics of the individual capable of leading a large organization is his willingness to find people who may (at least appear to) be more capable than the leader. (Of course, what really happens is that the leader gets the credit for being smart enough to find the smart people!)

Fourth, *delegate.* Find the people and then let them do what needs to be done. Certainly they will make mistakes. Didn't you? This needs to be done with care. You need to understand that delegation comes at various levels. We're not in favor of throwing people in the ocean to see if they'll sink or swim. It is appropriate to give a few swimming lessons ahead of time. But after the lessons, let them try it on their own.

Fifth, *ask the hard questions:* do you have the ability and the courage to move beyond where you are now? Has your own *lead-*

ership growth paralleled that of the organization? Are you utilizing the same style of leadership you had when the organization was much smaller? If you answer in the negative, then you have to do some hard questioning of where you belong and where the organization should be going.

Sixth, *make peace with yourself.* Perhaps you are not the person to lead this organization or local church to twice its present size of ministry. Maybe you need to accept the fact that you are much more gifted at running the smaller organization. That's easy to say and very difficult to do. But each of us is equipped to do God's perfect will for her or him. We can't tell you how to find God's will for your individual life, but the Bible assures us that God intends us to bring glory to him. Pleasing him is not dependent on your position in life but your willingness to use the gifts he has given you. How thrilling it is to see a mission executive step aside to let younger people move the organization ahead. What joy in heaven over a pastor who understands that God is calling him to a better role in a smaller congregation. (And what grace!)

Seventh, *educate others concerning what is happening.* Growth can be very discouraging. Since the larger the organization the more complex the challenges it must face will be, it is easy to forget how far the organization has come and how much we *do* know. Expect change. Be prepared for change. Help others to change and grow.

Organizations Are Different

God has so fitted us that we have different roles to play at different times. Growing in grace seems to require growing older and, we hope, wiser. Different needs require different organizations. Like people, organizations are unique. We do ourselves and others an injustice when we attempt to completely model our church or Christian organization after another. Organizations *are* different, and size is a major factor.

20 | Span
of
Control

HOW MANY INDIVIDUALS should report to the same person? How many and what decisions should lie with one another? What kinds of functions should report to the same leader? These are all questions that have to do with what is commonly known as "Span of Control." What follows are questions to consider, rather than specific directives.

How Many People?

How many individuals should report to one leader? There is no straightforward answer. Some individuals have exceptional ability to manage a large number of people, while others do much better with only a few. Some would feel completely lost if they only had three people working directly for them. Others feel overwhelmed by four or five. Still others feel comfortable with eight or ten. The answer to the question lies in both the ability and position of the individuals involved, the type of organizational structure, and the nature of the task.

Level of Position

Individuals who are responsible for the day-by-day, hour-by-hour quality performance of others are generally termed "supervisors." The assumption is that they are supervising the work output on a regular basis and that there will be a large number of technical questions which will have to do with the outcome and quality of the task. The supervisor is generally typified as having to spend the majority of his or her time dealing directly with employees. Examples would be the supervisor responsible for the mailing operation of a Christian organization or, in the case of a church, someone responsible for those preparing a church dinner for 200 people. Because the type of decisions and problems that arise are usually well within the experience of the supervisor, decisions can be made quickly, and the number of people who may be supervised is proportionally large. The fact that the supervisor is usually directly on hand where the work is being done also makes it more possible for the supervisor to oversee a large number of individuals. The supervisor then is typified by having a wide span of control. Supervisors are concerned with managing mental and manual skills of the staff.

At the other end of the managerial spectrum is the chief executive officer who is, by the nature of his task, responsible for a great deal of the future planning of the organization, concerned with the matters of policy, and overseeing the work of what Peter Drucker has termed "knowledge workers." Because of the nature of the executive's task, he or she must have a large amount of discretionary time. This means that there normally cannot be a constant flow of "interruptions" such as would be experienced by the first line supervisor.

Type of People

In general, the span of control will be influenced by the ability of the individuals reporting to the position and the degree to which work can be delegated to them. If there are a large number of new people or trainees, then the amount of time the executive will have to spend with each individual will normally be increased and the number of individuals who can be managed will be reduced.

Nature of the Task

There is a wide variety in the type and number of individuals required by an organization to carry out its work. For example, an organization involved in printing Christian literature might have many employees who are doing essentially the same type of work. The type of decisions faced by the different executives in the organization may not vary a great deal from day to day. On the other hand, another Christian organization, say a large overseas mission, may be involved with a wide variety of tasks encompassing everything from questions of theological understanding, translation of scripture, deployment of personnel, relationships with governments, and the movement of members of the organization and their families to different places around the world. The chief executive officer of the first organization might find that it was comfortable to handle ten or twelve different individuals reporting to him or her, while the head of the large mission might do better to have only four to six.

Staff and Line

Individuals who are directly responsible for the outcome of the organization are termed "line" people, while those responsible to assist someone in the performance of their particular management role are "staff" (see Chapter 18). For example, a personal secretary is staff to an executive. Sometimes the span of control of an executive is increased by actually adding the number of people reporting to him in the form of additional staff positions. These staff positions can be assigned to do the investigatory and study work and to assist the executive in coming to an understanding of the problems being faced.

Technical versus General Management

Some executives are involved with highly technical tasks, for example—the operation of a computing facility. The technical knowledge required is usually very high and the amount of time the executive will spend on problem-solving will necessarily be much greater than that of an executive who is responsible for a diverse number of tasks. The executive responsible for technical functions may consequently not be able to have as many people reporting directly to him or her.

What Functions Should Be Grouped?

The useful span of control of an executive will be greatly affected by the type of functions reporting to the position. If they are too diverse, the executive may have difficulty shifting quickly from one type of problem and/or decision to another.

Level of Delegation

The span of control is directly affected by the willingness and ability of the executive to delegate authority to his or her subordinates. If, for example, the organization is so arranged that each of its departments or committees can carry out their work against a set of determined goals and come to the responsible executive only when they are not reaching those goals, then it is possible to greatly increase the span of control. If, on the other hand, for reasons of concern on the part of the executive or unwillingness of the organization to delegate responsibility, then the executive will find himself faced with an increased number of day-to-day decisions; consequently, the number of decisions required by this executive will of necessity need to be reduced.

21 Bookkeeping and Accounting— an Introduction*

GOD HAS CALLED US to be good stewards of his wealth. Where do we begin? Leaders of young churches and new Christian organizations often have to set up the bookkeeping systems. Sometimes they even have to do the bookkeeping themselves until the organization grows. In the beginning, perhaps their "bookkeeping" was nothing more than some scribblings in a notebook. But for the Christian organization, particularly in the U.S. where tax exemption is important, eventually there will have to be a formal system.

Simplified bookkeeping textbooks and "introduction to accounting" books are useful self-instructional tools. Almost any junior college or adult education course could be taken to learn the basic principles. This chapter is an introduction. We hope it will help us to be more effective in our ministry.

When Does Bookkeeping Become Accounting?

B (Bookkeeping) comes before A (Accounting) in the alphabet of business management. Bookkeeping can exist alone without ever becoming accounting. But, to do an effective job, we need more than bookkeeping.

Bookkeeping is a history of the financial transactions of the

* This chapter was written by Alan W. Bergstedt, Director of the Financial Services Division of World Vision. Mr. Bergstedt is a CPA with many years experience both overseas and in the U.S.

organization. It is like a chronological record of news events without any integration. For example:

1. The L.A. Dodgers beat the Chicago Cubs 3 to 1 today.
2. The Dodgers scored sixty runs this past month.
3. The Dodgers' team batting average for the season is .261.

Of course there is a lot more that sports fans want to know about the Dodgers than mere facts like these. Relative league standings and other facts will help to provide an integrated picture of the success of the team and the challenges it faces for the rest of the season.

In the same way, accountants use the historical bookkeeping data and integrate it with annual goals and plans, financial budgets and management objectives in their reports to the leaders.

While a bookkeeper's task may be limited to historian or score-keeper, your organization could suffer by not including your accountant on the team of active players.

O.K.—but we have to start with a bookkeeping system. Right?

Yes, the money that is received and spent needs to be recorded in a more sophisticated way than do our personal cash, checking or credit card transactions. Organizations have to report on their finances to government, members, and boards. Consequently, systems have been designed to organize the transactions into condensed reports. The basic method used is the double entry bookkeeping system.

Why Is It Called a Double Entry System?

"Double entry" describes the principle that one transaction has an effect on two different groups of financial accounts. The groups of accounts are: *Assets* (e.g., Cash), *Debts or Liabilities* (e.g., Loans Payable), *Income* (e.g., Membership Fees or Donations) and *Expense* (e.g., Rent).

Let's look at a few illustrations of this double effect of transactions.

TRANSACTION	*EFFECTS*
Purchase of carbon paper	1. Decrease in Assets (Cash)
	2. Increase in Expense (Office Supplies)

Loan of $5,000 for new building	1. Increase in Assets (Cash)
	2. Increase in Debts (Loans Payable)
Down payment on building	1. Decrease in Assets (Cash)
	2. Increase in Assets (Buildings)
Mortgage contract for balance due on building	1. Increase in Assets (Buildings)
	2. Increase in Debts (Mortgage Payable)
Donations for new building	1. Increase in Assets (Cash)
	2. Increase in Income (Donations)

How Does This Get Organized into a System?

A bookkeeper needs a number of different journals in which to record all of these transactions, usually on a daily basis:

Cash Receipts Journal

Cash Disbursements Journal

Special Journals (i.e., Donations Journal or Subscriptions Journals)

General Journal

Then the bookkeeper transfers (posts) the amounts of the transactions in the two accounts that are affected. For example, for the $5,000 loan, the "Cash" account is increased by $5,000 and the "Loans Payable" account is increased by $5,000. These postings (entries) are called debits and credits to the accounts.

The system of accounts is called a "General Ledger." Each account is usually recorded on a separate ledger page.

The General Ledger is the tool of classifying the transactions in order to accumulate the total effects of the transactions on the accounts for a specific period of time. "Cash" may have increased to a new balance of $6,000 because of the $5,000 loan.

At the minimum, the bookkeeper should provide a list of all the accumulative balances of the accounts in the General Ledger whenever a report is due. This is called a "Trial Balance" because it tests to make sure that all the double entries have been made and that the General Ledger is in balance.

Then, further reports such as a "Balance Sheet" and a "Statement of Income and Expenses" can be prepared from the Trial Balance.

These special terms are a part of the bookkeeper's everyday terminology.

Should the Leader Learn the Bookkeeper's Language?

Leaders who do not have financial training should *not* have to learn this language. One of the roles of an accountant is to understand it and also know the language of the leaders of the organization. The accountant is the translator and interpreter to leadership and to the bookkeeper. An accountant may also fill the role of bookkeeper at times. But many organizations use an accountant to prepare the financial reports from the Trial Balance prepared by the bookkeeper.

Leaders can thus be more effective with an accounting system that goes beyond mere bookkeeping.

Leaders of established organizations need to understand the further benefits of interpretive accounting reports. Accounting is a means of integrating the leadership concerns of managing, planning, budgeting, and auditing.

What Can I Expect of Our Accountant?

When you have the feeling that you lack information from your bookkeeping system, you may need an accountant to design an accounting system which will meet your needs. This often requires reports to be developed which compare current year data with prior years and/or current year amounts with the budget.

Your accountant wants to serve you effectively. He or she needs to know what financial facts are critical to you. Each organization has some unique facts which are its most important measures of success.

An accountant can be helpful in designing an effective bookkeeping system which will produce the critical facts needed by the leadership for decision making. It is the accountant's responsibility to design the format of the financial reports so that these critical facts are clear to the leadership.

Readers of account reports should not have to dig through the reports to find the critical facts. These should be summarized in a "Highlights" page—the first page of a report, for example. Do you want to know how donations this month compare to last month? To the same month last year? Do you want to know the percentage of "faith promises" received to date? Make your need of critical facts known to your accountant, and he or she will highlight and monitor these facts for you.

How Many 'Critical Facts' Should We Watch?

Experience indicates that at any one time most of us can absorb up to ten critical facts. Since these are facts used for evaluation and future decision making, they may change from time to time and at different times of the year. Membership renewal income may be important in September and October, donations in December, and magazine subscription income in January.

Trends may be important to you or comparisons of certain income items to specific expense items may be critical. "Critical facts" are tools of decision making.

What Other Tools Could Be Used?

Graphs, charts and other visual means of reporting financial data should be a regular part of your financial reports. Trends and projections can be shown quite effectively on graphs.

Amounts should always be rounded off to the significant digits. Rarely is it necessary to include "cents" in a *report*. Often the nearest $100 or $1,000 is sufficient.

Be sure to focus on the year-to-date amounts as compared to budget, rather than just the current month amount. Columns for "Actual," "Budget," and "Difference" on your expense reports are helpful. Comparisons to the prior year amounts may also provide useful information for decision making. (Notice: this assumes you have a budget which, in turn, assumes you have done your planning).

For Further Reading

Bookkeeping Made Easy by Alexander L. Sheff is a single how-to-do-it book with practice problems and many illustrations. Paperback.

Financial and Accounting Guide for Nonprofit Organizations by Malvern J. Gross, C.P.A. is a thorough presentation of the theories, principles and procedures for bookkeeping, accounting, auditing, tax reporting, etc. for nonprofit organizations.

Managerial Accounting by S. Winton Korn and Thomas Boyd is a looseleaf 295 page self-study in accounting for nonfinancial managers.

22 What Is Overhead?

THERE IS ALWAYS a great deal of discussion about "overhead." It has been described as too high and too low. Some people think it is the cost of doing business. Others think it means the cost of fund raising or borrowing money.

How to Define It

Webster defines it as "business expenses not chargeable to a particular part of the work or product." So "overhead" is whatever *you* decide it is. Perhaps the idea comes from the fact that every organization which spends money has to have some place to work, a roof "overhead."

That roof initially costs something. And, whether you're paying rent or trying to write off the initial cost of the building, expense is involved. Consequently, when the time comes to balance the books, one is faced with the question, what does one do with the cost of the building which appears to have no *direct* bearing on what the organization is doing? How does one handle this expense "not chargeable to a particular product"?

If you are running a shoe store, and you pay a manufacturer $10 for a pair, how much should you add to the sales price for that roof overhead?

If you are a mission agency raising funds for a project overseas, how much should you add to your cost of fund raising because of that roof on the mission headquarters?

166

If you are a local church providing a weekly worship service in the same building as counseling, church school, and a Boy Scout troop, how much of that roof should be considered in anticipating the cost of having a worship service?

You have to decide. The roof, of course, is just one easy illustration of a number of costs that cannot be directly related to a specific ministry or product. We'll face more about what these other costs should be further along but, first, let us try to address the question of why one should set up a separate overhead account.

Why Have Overhead?

Because it makes accounting a great deal easier.

Suppose you have a small coffeehouse ministry in a storefront downtown. Everything that goes on in that building relates directly to the ministry: rent, heat, salaries, supplies, everything. You don't need to worry about overhead. Just add all those costs to the "coffeehouse ministry."

But suppose you share that building with three other ministries. One uses the building 8 hours a month, one 16, the third 32, the fourth 48. Suppose further that each ministry pays its own salaries and provides its own supplies. All that is used in common is the rented building, the heat, the janitor service and the wear-and-tear on the furniture.

How do we distribute the cost so that each ministry is paying its proportionate share? We figure out the cost of the total "overhead" (rent, heat, janitor, and wear-and-tear), and we apportion it proportionally according to the amount each ministry uses the building. By grouping all the overhead (nonspecific) costs together, we make accounting easier.

What Do You Include?

Anything you like, but usually costs that are common to most or all of the operations. In a large organization, this could mean that individual departments might have their own overheads as well as a total organization overhead.

For example, the senior pastor's, executive director's, or president's salary would oftentimes be considered overhead. So would an accounting department or a grounds service or anything used by everyone but difficult to count. It's hard to keep track of a receptionist's time. Make it overhead. It's quite simple to note copy machine costs. Don't make it overhead.

How Large Can It Be?

Unfortunately, for Christian organizations "overhead" has come to mean what we described in Chapter 17 as "process" cost. This is an unfortunate use of the term because, within certain limits, the size of an organization's overhead has nothing to do with its efficiency. An engineering company would not be surprised to have a 100 percent overhead. In other words, the costs it could directly assign to a project were equaled by nondirect costs. The large overhead is the result of investments in special scientific equipment, unpaid-for research, and so forth.

If the overhead gets to be 300 or 400 percent, this probably means that some of the direct costs are being counted as overhead, and should be made a part of the direct cost of the product or the service. Charging too many things to overhead means that people are really not concerned about the cost of what they are trying to accomplish.

How Do You Calculate It?

List all the items—such as rent, taxes, water, executive staff—that you decide cannot be easily related to a specific function, department or project. Add the yearly cost. That's your yearly *overhead*. All of these monthly expenses will be posted as debits to the overhead account as we described in the previous chapter.

How Do You Apply It?

Or, to put it another way, how do you distribute overhead expense to programs or projects? In the accounting terms of the previous chapter, our desire is that at the end of the year the overhead account should balance out to zero. How do we make that happen? That depends on the work you are doing. In a service-intensive organization, such as a mission or fund-raising ministry, it might best be divided up by the number of people working. Thus, if there were three departments with three people in one, five people in another, and seven people in the third for a total of fifteen people, one would distribute overhead on the basis of 3/15's, 5/15's and 7/15's.

In another case, it might be done on the basis of the amount of floor space used or the amount of dollars expended. On the basis of your estimate of how much your total *yearly overhead* will be, assign the appropriate portion to each function, department, ministry or project. This applied portion of overhead is known as *"burden."* The function, department, ministry or project has to "carry" this burden during the year.

You can then assign this burden once each year, as one-twelfth to be added each month, or you can assign it on an hourly, weekly or monthly part of salary. For example, to make bookkeeping simple, you might decide that a burdened hour of a clerk's time was to cost $6; $3 salary, plus $3 burden (share of overhead). This would mean that every time a clerk did one hour of work there was a $3 credit to the overhead account.

Suppose You Calculate Wrong?

The idea is to distribute all the overhead so that at the end of the year the overhead account is zero. But, suppose at the end of the year there is $1,000 left in the overhead account? You have what is known as $1,000 of *"under*-absorbed burden." Make a year-end accounting adjustment. That's much easier than trying to keep track all year of every change in cost.

Does This Have Anything to Do with Fund Raising?

Yes and no.

Fund raising is the cost of raising funds. If an organization decides that it is raising funds for many different projects, it will treat this cost of fund raising as an overhead expense. This is then *one* of the items that contribute to overhead, which for a ministry is part of the cost of administration (see Chapter 17).

What Do Christian Organizations Mean by Their Overhead?

Most of them mean the cost of doing business. In the case of a mission, this might mean what percentage of each dollar donated was used to insure that dollar was applied to the ministry for which it was intended. Since it is difficult to break out the cost of raising specific funds, all of the fund-raising costs usually have to be applied to the entire project and thus, for many people, end up as part of overhead.

The current trend is toward requesting not-for-profit agencies to show two costs: the cost of fund raising and the cost of administration. In this sense, it follows the input/process/output model already described in Chapter 17. "Input" is fund raising. "Process" is administration. "Output" is the ministry. Input plus process equals "overhead."

Do Most Christian Organizations Distribute This Overhead?

Unfortunately, no.

For example, few mission agencies break out the *total* cost of a program or project because they keep this overhead separate and don't "burden" the project. In many ways this tends to disguise the full cost of the project. Many field missionaries are resentful of the fact that the home office may withhold 10 percent of the funds given to the missionary to carry out the administration of these funds, which for many overseas missions might be described as overhead.

How Do You Compare Overheads?

With great difficulty.

Different types of organizations will have different costs of administration. It is usually less costly to raise funds for a project that has high emotional appeal than one which has low emotional appeal. Administering 100 overseas missionaries may require an entirely different kind of system than administering a relief project. Both may be carried out overseas, but the comparison may end there.

Is It Worth Tracking?

Yes, but on an internal basis and with *consistent accounting practice.*

If the accounting rules as to what constitutes administration (overhead) and what constitutes ministry vary from year to year, any comparison is meaningless. But assuming that the rules are maintained over a period of time, then any good manager will seek to maintain or reduce overhead, for in so doing he or she is allocating more funds to the ministry.

NOTE: The *rules* may be wrong. In our desire to keep overhead low, we may not do a good job of effectively applying the funds.

In other words, more administration may mean a more effective ministry. (Maybe.)

It Really Helps!

If you are trying to understand how to think of the effectiveness of your investment in God's kingdom through a particular Christian organization, you need to understand that an organization's "overhead" needs to be carefully explored before you compare it with another organization.

If you are a manager or executive in a Christian organization of any size or with multiple ministries, you need to understand the concept and the jargon. Elsewhere, Ted Engstrom has written: "Overhead is not a dirty word." It isn't. It's a viable concept or tool. Use it.

And as a manager, you will want to monitor your fund-raising and administrative costs from year to year as a part of your financial accountability to your donors.

For Further Reading

See Bergstedt's suggestions at the end of the previous chapter.

23	The
	Memo
	Game

THERE IS PROBABLY no form of organizational correspondence used or misused as much as the intraorganization or interoffice memo. How many times have you found yourself asking, "Now, why did he write *that*?" Or how many times have you ruefully wished that you had never started what has turned out to be some kind of a "memo war"? Christians are certainly not immune to this kind of misunderstanding.

Much has been written and many proverbs have arisen about the written word:

"Put it in *writing*!"

"If it's not in writing, it doesn't exist."

Writing Is Communication

Everyone knows it, but how often we forget that writing is just *one* form of communication and that writing alone seldom produces an adequate communication *system*. Relying on the written word for interaction with others cannot only generate misunderstanding, it can isolate us from the real world of people. It can build barriers to communication rather than channels.

The written word has significant weaknesses. How difficult it is for the reader to capture the real intention of a memo. How different it might have sounded if we could have heard the same account on the telephone or listened person-to-person.

Properly used, the written word is an extremely valuable tool. Improperly used, it can be wasteful at best, disastrous at worst.

Don't Use Memos for:

Complicated explanations. The chances are great that if the situation really is complicated, it will be misunderstood. Eventually, complicated procedures need to be reduced to writing to be understood. But we are not dealing here with writing procedures, but rather letters or memos between individuals.

Introducing new proposals. If it really is a *new* idea, your correspondents will usually need some prior background. To insure understanding we have to use the known (past) to explain the unknown (future).

Admonishing people. In a person-to-person conversation we always have the opportunity of qualifying or modifying what we have to say. We cannot only listen, but watch the reaction. Not so with a memo. It's like an arrow which, once launched, may land anywhere (and in anyone's hands). To make things worse, a hastily given reprimand may later prove to have been based upon inaccurate information, but the harm is already done.

Giving new orders. Even though you may have the authority, think twice before using it in a memo to issue orders in an unfamiliar area. You may discover that the recipient may misunderstand or does not believe you have the authority or may view it as you "throwing your weight around." This, in turn, can produce a whole flurry of counterproductive memos.

Use Memos for:

Detailed correspondence such as thank-you notes, making dates, confirming meetings, and so forth. It's usually faster than the telephone, and people can always write their response on the face of the memo.

Minutes of meetings. This is essentially a record of what has already been said and gives others a chance to agree or disagree.

Confirming a verbal order or action. Here again, the true communication has probably already taken place. The memo is used to transmit authority or to affirm something already agreed upon.

Confirming phone conversations. This can be a good strategy for making certain *you* have understood. Some leaders have found it a good procedure not to accept speaking engagements or large commitments on the phone. Rather, they ask their caller to spell out in writing what it is that is to be done. This gives them time to think and pray before accepting.

Giving affirmation or compliments. Just as the written reprimand really hurts, so the written compliment really blesses. It can be a quick handwritten note, or it can be at the beginning or the end of a larger memo. (By the way, this works *up* the line also. Don't forget to affirm your superiors when you feel they have done a good job.)

Communicating quickly to everyone at the same time. If you want to get information out to many people at about the same time, many times a duplicated memo is faster, and more likely to be accurate than the telephone. But note the cautions we've listed above.

Notes to yourself. Writing a message to yourself while you're thinking about it (or writing one "to file so-and-so") is an efficient time-saver and a good way to keep from forgetting things.

Make announcements of general interest or that need to be put in the record.

When you can't get through on the phone. Many leaders find it a good strategy to write a note asking for a decision and make sure the memo gets on the appropriate desk. It can save countless phone calls and many times permits the recipient to respond with a simple "OK" on the face of the memo.

Have a Correspondence Strategy

"Memos 101" is not found in the college curriculum. Make sure that people within the organization know what should be in writing and what should not.

Design a filing system. Most memos that follow the recommendations given above don't need to be filed. Perhaps you want to devise a system where any memo that is supposed to be filed is so indicated on the face of the memo. Where should the memo be filed? We devoted a whole chapter to this in our book, *The Art of Management for Christian Leaders.* The key thing to remember is that filing systems should be designed to *retrieve* things, not store them.

Are carbons of memos to be used for a follow-up system? Perhaps the secretary should keep a file of memos which require some action. Those can be reviewed periodically and a copy of the memo sent to those who need to be reminded that their response is overdue.

Teach People to Write Memos

Start with the date. It is amazing how many people fail to date their correspondence. This becomes particularly difficult when there is an exchange of memos between people and one wants to rebuild a history of events.

Don't forget your name! Many people find it helpful to have memo pads with their name imprinted on them. Many organizations, of course, have a standard memo form which has places for the date, addressee, addressor, and subject.

The purpose of a memo should be clear. Sometimes the best way to start is with a phrase like "I'm writing this so that . . . ." Many times an introductory paragraph will do the job.

Be as brief as possible and to the point. Work out the logic ahead of time. Some people find for a memo of any length the most useful thing is to first dictate or handwrite out all the items to be covered and then rearrange them in logical form.

Keep sentences short. Avoid lengthy paragraphs. This is the basic difference between written and spoken communication.

Enumerate or list. Many times it's helpful to enumerate or list the points you want to make. This can be done by subparagraphs that are numbered. Sometimes it is useful to use both headlines and subheadings.

Be clear as to who is to do what. If you expect a response to the memo, state from whom you expect it. A simple scribbled response on the memo can often be used in returning the message to the sender.

Avoid technical jargon wherever possible, particularly jargon that is not familiar to all of your readers. Use everyday, down-to-earth language. This is not to say that technical terms should not be used, only that your readers should understand them as well as you do.

Spell out the dates on which you expect the response or on which action items are required.

Avoid covering more than one subject in one memo. Write another memo for a different subject. This not only helps the correspondent but is very useful in keeping a filing or tracking system in order.

Differentiate between addressees and those who are to receive information copies. It should be assumed that only those to whom the memo is addressed will take action. If you want an action taken by the people to whom copies are sent, indicate that in the body of the memo.

Identify your memo as a response when responding to someone else's memo. Early in your memo indicate that this is a response. Many organizations include "refer to:" as part of the heading of their standard memo forms.

Avoid memo proliferation. It's always difficult to decide whether you're sending copies to too many people or leaving some off. Many people estimate their own status by what information they receive. Try to be clear both as to your own understanding and as to your organization's understanding of who should receive what.

Don't be a name dropper. Some managers use the leverage of their superior's position by writing to one of their peers and sending a copy to their superior. Make certain you are not doing this as an implied threat.

Handwrite your own memos. Don't always burden the secretary with typing a memo. Time can often be saved by writing your own memo as items occur to you.

Keep a memo pad available in your briefcase, car, nightstand, and other places. Write the memo as you think about it.

In Summation . . .

Remember that we are communicating with *people*. It takes their time to read what has been written. You are either helping or hindering them in performance of their work—making them either more or less effective people.

As you finish each memo or interoffice letter ask yourself the question, "Would I feel all right about receiving this memo, and would I understand the intention of the writer?"

To paraphrase the apostle, "Finally, brethren, whatever is true, whatever is honorable, whatever is just, whatever is pure, whatever is lovely, whatever is gracious, if there is any excellence, if there is anything worthy of praise, (write) about these things" (Phil. 4: 8).

For Further Reading

Writing for Results by David W. Ewing is an excellent one-volume summary.

24 | Managing Conflict

HOW DO WE MANAGE CONFLICT in a Christian organization? Or should Christian organizations, by definition, be free of conflict? Does the biblical concept of fitting in together disallow the presence of conflict?

What Is Conflict?

Call it "a difference of opinion," or whatever you like, conflict within organizations occurs whenever two or more people disagree on the solution to a problem or the value of a goal. There are two different opinions, two different ideas as to what should be done.

At first, "conflict" may seem like too strong a term. But behind every "battle of ideas" there are usually individuals. And since who we are and what we believe and stand for are intimately entwined, conflict does occur.

How such differences are resolved within an organization says a great deal about the style of leadership being exercised.

Is conflict permitted in your organization? How is it viewed? How is it resolved? How do you as a leader handle differences of opinion with your peers or subordinates? How do you view criticism (which is actually someone holding a different opinion than yours)?

For example, if you, as a leader, are experiencing very little conflict, very little difference of opinion, you have cause to suspect that you have an authoritarian style of leadership. If you seldom hear any criticism, it may well be that people are afraid to share it.

At the other end of the spectrum is the laissez-faire style of leadership which handles conflict by insisting that others settle their differences among themselves and refuses to intervene.

How Do We Respond to Conflict?

How we respond to conflict reflects both our view of ourselves and our view of conflict. It will also depend upon our view of power and its use.

Every leader is empowered because of his or her position. Influence is power. Resources are power. The ability to give directions is power. Prestige and reputation are power. In this sense, power is not a bad word, it is just a way of suggesting that some people are in a position because of a situation or because they have more influence on the world than others.

If we view conflict as a contest in which one person wins and another loses, it may well be we have a need to win so that we can accumulate power. If we view conflict as an arena in which creativity can flourish and new ideas emerge, there then will be less of a drive toward personal power.

When a leader uses the position of leadership to win an argument or to overrule a subordinate, individuals within the organization quickly sense that conflict is being resolved by the use of power. They, in turn, will either attempt to accumulate power for themselves or avoid conflict.

If, on the other hand, they see that differences of opinion are welcomed and that ultimate decisions are made on the basis of available data and an analysis of the overall situation, they are less likely to accumulate power to themselves by becoming winners of arguments.

Conflict and Creativity

There is a close relationship between conflict and creativity. To avoid conflict is to inhibit creativity. When we adhere strictly to the status quo, we usually avoid conflict, but we also eliminate the need for finding new or more appropriate solutions. It is in the press of the struggle for change that the creative juices start to flow.

Almost everyone begins life with a high degree of creativity. Through the process of enculturation we learn to conform, to suppress our creative urges. A few of us fight this push toward conformity and are usually branded different, artistic or even bohemian. The rest of us must wait for a "safe" environment before we will risk being creative. Conflict then becomes a catalyst to creativity. "Iron sharpens iron."

If we were working with unthinking machines or talking about the forces of nature, there would be no need to discuss "conflict." Conflict has to do with people. When an individual or a group sets out to change things, conflict is inevitable. It need not be destructive.

Win-Win versus Win-Lose

Remember the old joke about "Heads I win—tails you lose"? In a trite way it reflects a view of interpersonal relationships. Life is seen as a contest in which some win and others lose. The "winners" get to the "top." The "losers" never make it.

At the opposite pole from such a win-lose picture of life is "win-win." How good it feels to describe a situation in which "everybody wins." For most of us, such experiences happen all too seldom.

This need not be so. There is a style of leadership which actively promotes situations in which both parties win. There are ways of managing conflict that view it as not only useful but necessary, and at the same time insist that it need not be destructive.

Win-Win Management Style

What kind of management style permits creative conflict which produces feelings of "winning" in both parties?

Begin with clear, high performance goals (there is that word again!). If there is no standard against which to measure the usefulness of a decision, the solutions will tend to be subjective and personal. If no one has stated where it is that we are going, there will be little agreement on how we will get there.

Share information up and down the organizational structure. Bad data produces bad decisions which usually produce bad feelings.

Surveys of felt need among members of organizations indicate the need to know what is going on and to feel like one is "in the know." This is usually near the top of the list. What people don't know *can* hurt them, for when people don't know something they believe is important to them, they will usually find "answers" either from others or from their own analysis of the situation. This usually results in the question, "Why aren't *they* telling me?"

Model appropriate problem-solving approaches. If the leadership makes unilateral decisions or uses its position to win arguments, the rest of the organization will attempt to do the same.

We are not discussing here the question of who must *ultimately* decide. In Harry Truman's words, "The buck stops here." The leader must eventually make what is often a lonely decision. Rather, we're talking about *problem-solving,* the attempt to find our way forward past a difficult situation in which we need all the information we can get and need to hear as many appropriate opinions as are available.

Model a listening ear. A great deal of emotion is spent in attempting to be heard. If I don't believe you understand my position, how can I accept yours? Too often the aggressive, bright leader will see exactly where someone is going in the discussion and, with a desire to save time (the leader's and the speaker's), will interrupt with a, "I understand, but . . . ." Seldom will the speaker *feel* that he or she has been heard.

Focus on facts, not emotions. This is a key idea. We are all very much aware of how easy it is to carry the day with an appeal to the emotions. Christian organizations and Christian leaders can unknowingly become manipulative by appealing to loyalty, "the cause," or biblical ideals which may have little bearing on the problem at hand. The facts, to the extent they are known, paint one picture. But it is not the picture we would really like to see. "Like" is an emotional word, and too often we convert these emotions into rhetoric that has little to do with facts.

Give training in group problem-solving. Many people resort to a bulldozer style of settling differences because that's the only way they know.

Most of us assume that the way we feel is the way everyone else feels. The way we have learned to handle our problems is probably the way everyone else has learned to handle their problems. It is usually a *learned* experience if there are different styles, different responses for different situations.

Managing Conflict

The business of making decisions in an organization is going on all the time. Many decisions are made by individuals without consulting anyone. Often there is no recognition that a decision *has* been made. But in the midst of all this there will be discussions, debates, problem-solving sessions in which more than one opinion vies for acceptance. The goal of management is to encourage debate but discourage win-lose situations. How is that done?

Insist on facts, or at worst, clearly differentiate between facts and opinion: "Tom, I can see that you really feel very strongly about this. But, would you first list for me all of the *facts* on which we all agree? Then we can go on to the opinions."

View problems as a deviation from a goal. What is the goal to which this problem relates? The task of the group then becomes to discover solutions that enable the goal rather than enhance an individual: "Bill, I'm not sure exactly what this problem is that you're trying to describe. Help me out here. What is the goal you're trying to reach and what is keeping you from reaching that goal?"

Break down the problem-solving process. Take it one step at a time. Make sure that you and others understand the difference between these steps:

Begin with data gathering. What are the facts? What information do we have? What are additional data that we need to gather?

Once you have as many facts as you can accumulate (or as you have time to gather) move on to the various alternative solutions. Seek as many possible solutions as you have time for.

There will be tradeoffs between these solutions. Some will have pluses as well as minuses. Try to see the positives and the negatives of each solution.

Move on to integrating these various solutions into a working compromise (compromise is *not* a bad word).

Too often we force agreement on one solution, or a part of a solution, before we have adequately explained and examined alternatives. At other times, we hold one solution over and against another, rather than seek the best features of both.

Seek to strengthen the power of the group. The opposite side of that coin is to avoid enhancing the power of one contestant. Keep asking the question, "How can this problem (conflict) be used to everyone's benefit?" Most of us are familiar with the idea that every problem should be seen as a challenge. Take that a step further: every problem should be seen as an opportunity.

Agree to agree. The primary tool of the labor arbitrator is to obtain agreement from both parties that mutual agreement is possible and will eventually occur.

Let's not confuse our *theological* positions here. We are not suggesting that we ask people to agree to depart from the fundamentals of what they believe. What we are speaking to here is the everyday business of working out solutions in the organization.

Promote listening. We haven't been heard until the other person can accurately state our view. This takes time, patience, and a sense that the individual is just as important as the issue at hand.

Conflict and the Christian

Conflict, in whatever shape or form it may appear, should be faced and used creatively, and accepted as part of the personal and organizational maturing process. We will always have it, it will always be present, and we must recognize its dangers as well as opportunities.

The two Chinese characters making up the word for "crisis" are "danger" and "opportunity." This is what conflict presents to us—danger in making errors, in how we handle it, and opportunity for moving solidly ahead.

Christians in Christian organizations, and particularly the local church, have a unique advantage in working through conflict. There is a confidence that the God who knows the end from the beginning will bring about equitable solutions as we submit our hearts and wills to him and the leadership of his Holy Spirit.

This is a magnificent "plus" for the Christian. Remember, you and I—plus God—always represent the majority.

Management styles differ from individual to individual and from organization to organization, but for Christian leadership the promised help and guidance of the Holy Spirit can always be asked for, accepted, and trusted. Be sure, early on in conflict resolutions, to seek the wisdom which God promises us in James 1.

Interpersonal Relations

Within an organization the interpersonal relations aspect of conflict is of prime importance. Ted has discussed this in his book, *The Making of a Christian Leader:*

> The proper handling of troublesome situations demands both tact and the ability to handle people. This requires taking the action needed to deal with basic reasons behind stress and conflict. Problems with people will not become large if you keep them little ones. To do that you must act quickly and directly when the slightest tension begins to surface between individuals.

Tact may be defined as intuitive perception. It is insight and decorum that is fit and proper in a given situation that helps to avoid giving offense. For example, a tactful person is able to reconcile two opposing views without compromising his own principles. Tact means that a person has a sensitivity to other people; whereas others might wound or hurt, he is able to use the same words or approach with a slightly different emphasis or phrasing that does not offend.[1]

Every human being experiences tension, frustration, and conflicts with other people. If he does not, he is either psychotic or withdrawing from the mainstream of life. A mark of maturity is the ability to handle conflict. This includes the ability to deal with realities as to what can and cannot be changed. A mature executive said to me, "I have learned never to fret over something that I cannot change." Such an approach to life is evidence of stability. The ability to make those necessary compromises with what cannot be changed largely determines whether one will be successful as a social being.[2]

. . . The way a person deals with conflict does denote whether he is a strong, healthy, emotional person, or one who develops neurotic symptoms.[3]

It's Hard Work

But it's worth it. If you and your organization have been operating on the basis of a top-down, do-it-my-way style, it will take some time before people will believe that you really want honesty and openness. If this has been your style, be ready for some painful pricks to your ego.

But if current management research is not enough to persuade you to try some new approaches to managing conflict, read again the twelfth chapter of 1 Corinthians. How surprising that the world finds profitable what the Holy Spirit has been saying to us for almost 2,000 years!

For Further Reading

We recommend *New Ways of Managing Conflict* by Rensis and Jane Gibson Likert.

---

[1] Ted W. Engstrom, *The Making of a Christian Leader* (Grand Rapids: Zondervan Publishing House, 1976), p. 191.

[2] Ibid., p. 86.

[3] Ibid., p .87.

25 | Where Do You Draw the Line?

EVERY ORGANIZATION HAS its own style, its own way of doing things. Much of how it carries out its day-to-day business is based on a set of rules, many of which are never put down in writing. Some of these might be classified as traditions: Who gets copies of what memos? What are the rules about entering someone's office with or without speaking to his secretary? Who takes the lead in inviting whom to lunch? Is it all right to make personal phone calls on church or company time? Who pays for them? Does everyone take the same amount of time for lunch, or is it all right for some people to take a greater amount of time?

Where Do You Draw the Line?

How do we sort out which rules apply to whom? The Christian organization has a particularly difficult time in answering the question. On the one hand is the responsibility of individuals to fulfill their roles according to the expectations and requirements of the organization. On the other hand is the commitment the members of the organization have to one another, a reflection of their common commitment to God in Christ.

After all, Christianity is all about *how we live*. After the doctrinal foundation of the first eleven chapters of Romans, Paul exhorts us to God-honoring relationships, relationships so personal that we are described as "all joined together to each other as different parts of one body" (Rom. 12: 5 TEV).

"Love must be completely sincere. Hate what is evil, hold on to what is good. Love one another warmly as Christian brothers, be eager to show respect for one another. Work hard. Do not be lazy. Serve the Lord with a heart full of devotion. Let your hope keep you joyful, be patient in your troubles, and pray at all times. Share your belongings with your needy fellow Christians and open your homes to strangers" (Rom. 12: 9–13 TEV).

How Do We Interpret This for the Organization?

As we have pointed out before, for the local church, the question is never resolved. It can never be a question of the local church before the individual or the individual before the church. Somehow we have to find a way of meeting the needs of both. And yet for the organization created to work outside of the structure of a local fellowship, it seems obvious that the organization has been called into being to *do* something. If it fails to do this, it loses its reason for existence.

But the dilemma remains. Are some people given more freedom than others? Do some have more prerogatives than others? What is best for the organization? What is best for the individual? Where *do* you draw the line?

Pieces of the Puzzle

It is a complex situation. We can only make a start at laying out some of the factors:

For example, in the state of California the law states that there are two classes of employees: exempt and nonexempt. An exempt employee does not receive overtime pay since it is expected that this person operates at an "executive level." It is assumed that this person will keep working until the job is done. On the other hand, the nonexempt employee must be paid on the basis of a 40-hour week. If this person is unable to finish his work during the day, and he is asked to keep working, he must be paid an additional amount.

But is this the only distinction between these two groups? Is there no difference between a person who enters the organization as a junior clerk and another person who has faithfully served the organization for ten years and is now a senior secretary? Should not the older employee receive more "benefits"? But, how *can* we treat each person as an individual and still be "fair"?

What right does the organization have to motivate its employees to do much more work for the same salary because they are engaged in the "cause of Christ"? The leaders, or senior executives, may have founded or joined the organization because they believed in the cause of which it was a part. On the other hand, that junior clerk who joined the organization two weeks ago may have only been looking for a job and liked the idea of working in a "Christian environment."

What can the Christian organization expect of its staff that a non-Christian organization cannot? On the other hand, what should Christians expect of the Christian organization over and above the non-Christian organization?

What about the differences in pay? Should the leaders of the organization be paid the same salary as the most junior person who started two weeks ago? If this is not the case, should salaries in Christian organizations be the same as those in non-Christian organizations?

Working on the Puzzle

Ultimately, each organization will have to answer these questions for themselves. But there are some factors which need to be understood. These are not answers, just data to help reach your own (probably temporary) solution:

—There is something in human nature that says the wants of yesterday become the needs of today. What starts as a "benefit" given by the organization soon becomes a "right" of the employee. For example, one year an extra half day is allowed the staff before a holiday because of a special situation. The following year it is "suggested" that this would be nice to do again. By a third year it is "understood" that an extra half day will be given each year.

—There are few secrets within an organization. If a benefit is given to one person, it will soon be expected by others.

—There is no longer a willingness on the part of Westerners in general, and Western Christians in particular, to walk to someone else's agenda. Young men and women today feel that they have the right to ask "Why?" Older leaders have a particularly difficult time with what they regard as either rebelliousness or laziness on the part of young people. Whether these changing attitudes are right or wrong is not the question here. It is important that we understand the changing culture within which we live.

—There is a growing Western tendency to view the work one does to "earn a living" as only that. If this interferes with "my life," it is the former that must change. In other words, employers are being asked to shape their jobs to the individual life style desired by the individual.

—How this jibes with the Protestant work ethic, which most of us have come to believe is fundamental to our effectiveness, remains to be seen. Some Christians view this change with a great deal of alarm and concern, while others see it as a rightful return to priorities that make the value of persons more important than the value of accomplishments.

—There will always be a "generation gap" in the ability of an organization to explain itself and its actions to its employees. The young church secretary, fresh out of school and buried under what appears to be an ever-increasing stack of letters, may never understand why the pastor spends an hour and a half at lunch. It is always difficult to see the beauty of the top of the mountain when one is buried at the bottom.

—As we discussed in Chapter 2, everyone has three kinds of time: leader-imposed time, over which we have no control; peer-imposed time, over which we have little control; and discretionary time, that which is left over. It is in the nature of task-oriented organizations that those at the "bottom" have very little, if any, discretionary time, while those at the "top" have a great deal. However, this idea is not understood and little appreciated by many people.

—There is a great difference in the value of the individual's time at the ends of the organizational spectrum. The chief executive's time may be worth (to the organization) $100 per hour while the junior clerk's may be $5 per hour. Salaries seldom reflect (particularly in Christian organizations) this difference. But again, this difference in value is not understood by most people.

—As a result of this difference in the value of time between individuals, most organizations have perquisites that are designed to give organizational leaders more time, or more effective use of their time. These vary from assigned parking spaces to longer vacations. The apostles evidently faced the same kind of a situation. We read in Acts 6: 2: "It is not right that we should give up the preaching of the word of God to serve tables. ... we will devote ourselves to prayer and to the ministry of the word."

—This is seldom understood by younger members of an organization. Some leaders easily succumb to the idea that they should be willing to do anything that any member of their organization can do.

—Some organizations see all staff members as joining a cause. As a result, there is a tacit assumption that since everyone is equal in the sight of the Lord, that everyone is equal. Others require only the leadership to hold the vision. There is a great difference in these two kinds of organizations.

What Should the Staff Member Expect of the Christian Organization?

A defined ethos: Are you a movement or a company? Are you starting out on the assumption that before a person joins your organization he/she must be as completely dedicated to the cause as its leader? Or are you satisfied to have some members who are just "employees"? Your staff needs to know before they join the organization.

Dedication to the task, demonstration by the leadership that they are about the most important of all businesses, God's business. This will work itself out in many different ways, but it must be there.

Persistence, a doggedness about getting the job done.

A clear statement of purpose and goals, with a good understanding of how individuals at different levels relate to those goals.

Christian ethics: "Love is patient and kind; is not jealous or conceited or proud; love is not ill-mannered or selfish or irritable; love does not keep a record of wrongs; love is not happy with evil but is happy with the truth. Love never gives up; its faith, hope and patience never fail" (1 Cor. 13: 4–7 TEV).

Good stewardship, the thoughtful concern about how finances and individuals are used. There is nothing more devastating to the staff of a Christian organization than to believe that the Lord's money is not being used wisely and well.

Openness, an earnest attempt to spell out the boundaries of its methods of operations and its expectation of individuals.

What Should the Christian Organization Expect of the Christian?

Diligence and competence in work, a desire to do better. This may be bounded by the forty-hour week or by job descriptions.

We are not speaking here of how long a person works, but the attitude with which they approach the task.

Uprightness and integrity in the use of time, company supplies and equipment, expense accounts and level of conversation. How easy it is to fall into the trap of, "Everyone else does it, why shouldn't I?"

Continual effort to maintain Christian attitudes. Calmness. Reluctance to take vengeance. Little complaining and chronic griping. A level of trust toward one another.

Warm and responsible interpersonal relationships, a sensitivity to the use of power or position, an avoidance of exploiting people, a sensitivity to the suffering that goes on around us and a willingness to help in time of need at the point of felt need.

A response to the organization norms. Conformance to the rules.

How to Draw the Line

Decide if you are a "movement" or a "company." A movement needs to clearly define the goal to which it is calling its members.

Realize that in our modernizing society, *we are always in the process of change.* Rules and norms appropriate two years ago may no longer be appropriate today. Dress code is a good example. In 1970, we worried about dresses too high above the knee. In 1976, we were concerned about dresses too close to the floor.

Stay abreast of secular standards in your community, everything from changes in the cost of living to appropriate dress.

Spell out rules and norms in writing to the best of your ability. Even for the small organization a staff handbook covering things like the organization's history, statement of faith, basic objectives, financial policies, requirements and procedures, salary administration, hours, attendance, benefits, vacations, holidays, anything that has become a uniform policy, is helpful.

Train your supervisors regarding what it means to be a good supervisor and the inevitable tensions of living and working.

Be open to question and challenge, but be consistent in response. Have times to regularly remind the staff of the rules, perhaps coupled with a time for seeking suggestions or improvements. For example, in our own organization, we periodically have staff retreats in which we invite the staff to submit anonymous written questions on any subject they like. We make a point of reading *all* the questions in attempting to answer them.

Attempt to explain the difficulty in applying uniform rules and regulations and the need for flexibility. Be flexible where needed. At the same time, be ready to announce your mistake if you have gone too far in giving benefits to one person that you are unable to give another.

Keep the cause to which Christ has called you clearly before all members of the organization. Report on successes and failures. Share in prayer (we'll devote a whole chapter to this at the end of this book).

26 | Dangers

ORGANIZATIONS SUCCEED OR FAIL for many different reasons. When they are young, and the future is bright and exciting, it is easy to miss some of the pitfalls that lie ahead in the road. But the mature organization is not without its hazards. In many ways the dangers that it faces are more subtle. They are often the result of success rather than failure. In what follows we have attempted to list ten dangers for the Christian organization. You can use the checklist at the end to help you discover whether you may be facing any of them.

It has been well said that an organization begins with a *man*, becomes a *movement* that develops into a *machine* and eventually becomes a *monument*. How do those things happen?

Settle for the Status Quo

How easy it is for the Christian agency to be willing to settle for the status quo, to struggle to "keep things as they are." But it is impossible for any organization to stand still. They will either progress or retrogress. God's work demands that we move forward. This is true in our personal life. It is just as true in our organizational life. Once we settle for maintaining things as they are now, at that moment we begin to slide toward ineffectiveness, a slide which becomes steeper the farther we go.

As we pointed out in Chapter 23, one of the clues that we are settling for the status quo is lack of internal tension within the organization. This naturally leads us to the next danger.

Eliminate Creative Tensions

The organization which has "made it" tends to resist creative tensions. We like to settle for peace and calm. Creative people have new ideas. They want to change things, to make things better. But new ideas bring with them a conflict of interest, and conflict of interest brings internal tension. When a new idea is offered, too often what we hear is, "You have done things wrong," rather than "Here's a better way."

The result of eliminating creative tension is that we often fail to face up to the situation around us. An example of this might be how we handle the world economic scene with its increasing inflation. If we do not go through the struggle of creatively addressing ourselves to the tensions this is going to create in our ministries at home and abroad, many organizations will find themselves in deep difficulty down the road.

Don't Plan in Depth

Almost every organization does some planning, but if we fail to plan our ministries in depth, as well as breadth, danger lies ahead. In other words, it is too easy for us to look for quantity and size as a primary result of our planning, rather than quality and meaningfulness in the program and ministry God has placed before us. These need to be placed in priority. Quality is far more important than quantity. Size must always be secondary to the effectiveness of ministry which we perform under God.

Discriminating between breadth and depth is not easy. That is why there is a real danger here. We may have a great desire to expand our ministry throughout and beyond our community or to the rest of the world, but if the quality of ministry that we are performing at the place we have begun is not being continually strengthened, then we may discover that we have overextended ourselves.

Stop Listening

A subtle danger for experienced Christian leaders is a failure to really hear and listen to younger colleagues, to give them a role in participatory leadership. Younger staff members have a great deal to contribute. Often we are so certain that we have "been there" before that we do not hear them. This is even more true of our usual attitude toward younger women staff members. Those who are older and who provide leadership need to have an open heart to what younger colleagues may say as God speaks to them.

After all, it is self-evident that tomorrow's leadership rests with them. If we want to insure the continuation of a solid ministry, then we need to invest ourselves in developing leadership. Part of the investment is to have the time and the skill to listen.

Depend on Past Successes

How easy it is to place our confidence in what the organization has done in the past, or even in what it is doing now. It is easy to bask in the accolades of others who tell us what a great job we have done. But our dependency is not on what we have accomplished in the past or what we are doing now; rather it should be on the work and ministry of the Holy Spirit. How wonderful it is to cast ourselves upon him and believe that he will lead us on a miracle basis.

How do you do that? We are the first ones to admit that it is a paradox. On the one hand, we are responsible for God's work. On the other hand, God is doing it all. But when we place our confidence in what we have done in the past and fail to balance this with complete confidence in what God will do in the future, danger lies ahead.

Depend on Our Personal Experience

This is a corollary to depending upon the organization's experience. Too many of us are ready to depend upon our own brain power, expertise, and experience, rather than to depend upon God. Obviously, God has gifted those in the church, and these gifts need to be utilized and sharpened. But it is God who "is at work in you, both to will and to work for his good pleasure" (Phil. 2: 13). We must constantly be reminded that it is "not by might, nor by power, but by my Spirit, says the Lord . . . " (Zech. 4: 6).

Another way of saying this is there is a danger of our attempting to take back what we have given to the Lord, to take back the management of our lives into our own hands.

Neglect the Highest Good

Here is a danger of which we are all aware but too seldom face. It is the danger of becoming so busy in what are genuinely good and fine works for the Lord that we neglect the highest good, which is our worship of God through all of our service. We need to saturate our hearts with God's Word. How easy it is to become so busy about his business that we forget God's desire is for us to know him.

We need to remember that it should be "my utmost for his highest."

Forget Unity

Christian organizations have both the promise and the demand of a special kind of unity. We are related to one another as the different parts of a body. This relationship is not an option. It is a command. The maintenance of this type of Christian unity takes skill and perseverance. Too easily we forget that the primary way the world is going to know that we are Jesus' disciples is by the love we have for one another. And the world will believe Jesus is the Christ when they see that we have the same type of oneness with the Father that he had (John 17).

Unity is not the absence of healthy conflict caused by creativity and differences of opinion. Unity finds its first dimension in the allegiance we have to our Savior. It finds its expression in our recognition that each of us has gifts which help us to function as parts of this body. Part of our task is to affirm one another's gifts and to respect one another's roles. This is a primary task of Christian leadership.

To Lose the Joy of Service

How quickly those who are in the work, who are on the front line of service, can lose the real joy of that service. Paradoxically, the further we proceed in positions of leadership and authority, the greater servants we should become. The highest role of leadership is that of servant. It is said of our Lord that he came not to be ministered unto but to minister.

Christian leaders, like all leaders, need to be undergirded with authority and perquisites of office. However, if these are seen as being the just due of the *individual,* rather than the accoutrements of the office, we can come dangerously close to believing that we are the ones who should be served.

The servant role ought to mark us. This kind of ministering service brings the deepest joy, gratification, and satisfaction.

Forget the Bottom Line

Accountants like to call our attention to the "bottom line," the final statement of what is left over after outgo has been balanced off against income. The bottom line in Christian service is the complete honoring of Christ and offering to the world the knowledge of the Savior. Every organization needs to know what is its "bottom line." Everything must head toward this objective.

A 'Danger Ahead' Checklist

Here are ten questions that relate to the ten dangers we have given you. Note that none of them are bad in themselves. In fact, they may be very good. However, if you check three or more of these as being characteristic of your organization, perhaps it is time to evaluate. Perhaps you have already succumbed to some of the dangers we have outlined above.

(   ) Our organization chart hasn't changed in the past twelve months.

(   ) I haven't been faced by a new creative idea in the past two weeks.

(   ) We have no way of measuring the quality of our programs against a set of standards.

(   ) Most of our executives are fifty or over.

(   ) There is a great sense of satisfaction in the organization and all that God has accomplished through the organization in the past.

(   ) Most of the leaders of the organization have a real sense of being on top of their jobs.

(   ) Few of the leaders in our organization are what one would call real Bible students.

(   ) The average person in our organization would question whether we have true biblical unity.

(   ) Most of our leaders think that the primary function of leadership is to lead.

(   ) We seldom ask the question as to whether the ministry we are performing is there for the *primary* purpose of honoring God.

27 | When Is It Time to Pray?

IT IS APPROPRIATE that we end this book with a call to prayer. We live in an increasingly complex world. More and more we have a sense of impotency both as individuals and organizations. Too often we quietly ask ourselves, "What difference do we make anyway?"

But in such a world-gone-out-of-control the Christian organization has a special advantage. Because we believe in a God who stands outside the creation, because we believe *his* purpose will ultimately be accomplished, we can rest in the confidence that we *do* make a difference. We are part of a much greater "plan." Just because we cannot clearly comprehend how all we do will ultimately work together for good does not dissuade us from believing that we are plugged into the Source of all life.

Thus we can believe in prayer, we can call one another to prayer. We can make prayer an integral part of our daily lives. For we believe that prayer is the medium through which we carry on conversations about the business in which we are involved.

Christian Organizations Are Different

There is, or there should be, something different about Christian organizations. It is not enough that an organization have Christian purposes. There is a basic assumption that the leadership of this organization owes its first allegiance to God in Christ. Therefore, though we realize that most "Christian organizations" are those who are about some specifically defined Christian task, our primary qualification for Christian organizations is the relationship of its staff to Jesus Christ as Lord.

Suppose one had the opportunity to continuously observe the *behavior* of the individuals within the Christian organization? What would one discover? Should not one come to the conclusion that these indeed are Christians? Is not the tree most easily identified by the fruit it bears?

What Behaviors Should We Expect?

On a horizontal level, on the level of our relationships with all men, the Bible calls us to love. The measure of one's commitment to Jesus Christ is the gauge of this relationship. "By this all men will know that you are my disciples, if you have love for one another" (John 13: 35). So in a Christian organization one should expect to observe acts of love, acts which demonstrate such a relationship.

In the vertical dimension one would expect to find acts of prayer, times of praise, petition, thanksgiving, and intercession which demonstrate that the individuals within its organization see themselves as part of a dimension much greater than themselves.

The Mystery of Prayer

It is not our purpose here to attempt to define prayer, or even to justify it in the life of the Christian. We are *called* to pray (Jer. 33: 3); we are *commanded* to pray (Col. 3: 17).

At the same time, we need to understand the mystery of prayer. On the one hand, although we are asked to pray about everything, this does not excuse us from being responsible nor from attempting to be effective managers. On the other hand, the fact that we are doing an excellent job of leadership and management does not reduce the need or the demand for prayer.

The mystery is much like that of the sovereignty of God and the freedom and responsibility of man. The Bible states categorically that God is completely sovereign and will give his glory to no man. It states just as categorically that men have freedom and responsibility to act. Any attempt to bridge these two concepts intellectually is bound to fail. But as any mature Christian can testify, if one lives as though both were equally true, the results demonstrate that they are.

For reasons known only to the mind of God, prayer is always God's *modus operandi,* not only in our personal lives but in our organizations as well.

What Happens in the Organization?

Unfortunately, many of us can also testify to the fact that within our organizational life prayer has become a sterile thing at best. Too often it is almost formalized into a certain cultural role within an organization. Meetings may be opened or closed with prayer. There are set times when people are called upon to pray. To many, prayer is viewed as a duty imposed by the organization, rather than the natural response of the individual within the organization.

Perhaps even worse is the secret feeling of embarrassment we may have as executives and leaders in Christian organizations that others will think our desire to pray is just something we feel forced to do as part of our position.

When Is It Time to Pray?

The obvious answer is that it is always time to pray. Every successful leader in the Bible was an individual who recognized the importance and value of prayer.

We need to petition God for guidance and wisdom as well as blessings upon decisions that we have made. Praise should be continual.

Prayer is probably the single most important factor of uniting hearts together in a ministry.

Prayer is a statement of belief, a statement of faith. It acknowledges that our times are not in our own hands. It is not a substitute for decisions, nor the substitute for planning. Note that James does not condemn the planning of those who say "Today or tomorrow we will go into such and such a town and spend a year there and trade and gain." Rather, he wants people to acknowledge that the future is in the Lord's hands: "Instead you ought to say, 'If the Lord wills, we shall live and we shall do this or that'" (James 4: 13–15).

Where to Begin?

It is the responsibility of Christian leadership to model a life of prayer. This is true both in the personal life of the executive and the way staff associates are called to prayer with regularity and frequency.

We *need* to begin with formal times of prayer together. There *should* be a specified time at least once each week when the entire staff of a Christian organization within a given locality comes together to acknowledge themselves as Christians, to worship the Lord and to pray together.

But there needs to be something beyond this. In the paragraphs that follow, we describe some of the approaches with which we have had experience.

A Weekly Time Together

There is nothing sacred about coming together weekly, but it does seem that coming together as an organization within the context of a week of Christian life gives a spiritual rhythm and heartbeat to an organization. We are not suggesting that such a once-a-week gathering should be always devoted exclusively to prayer. Prayer should certainly be a part of such a time and there will be some times when we will want to spend the whole time praying together, perhaps corporately, perhaps by breaking up into smaller groups.

Certainly this is the time to share the needs of the organization or church and to demonstrate that we believe "prayer changes things," and particularly matters pertaining to our organization.

A Daily Group Devotional

By having staff gather in small groups of four to fifteen it is possible to give opportunity for a wide range of worship and prayer experiences. There is always the danger that such a regular meeting can become mere routine. Consequently, it is necessary to use your creative imagination in designing the program. One of the best ways of doing this is to have members of the staff involved in planning the kind of experiences they would like to have. This responsibility can be rotated within the group. Perhaps planning ahead a month is useful.

Prayer Partners Are Helpful

By pairing up individuals as prayer partners within the organization for a week or a month you give opportunity for more in-depth praying and sharing. Experience shows that this, too, can become no more than a formal nod toward prayer involvement. This tendency can be overcome by encouraging people to share prayer requests, get together for lunch, or have a coffee break together.

If you do establish such a system, it is also important that someone be made responsible for it.

Circulate Prayer Requests

These can come not only from within the staff, but also from outside the immediate staff. Whether you are a local church or a Christian service agency, there will always be those whom you know who need to be brought before the throne of grace. By specifically asking people to pray, you sharpen their own awareness of their own need.

Special Time of Extended Prayer

It would seem almost self-evident that the organization attempting to be sensitive to its role as part of the kingdom of God should discover times when the most appropriate response is to put aside all normal business and have an extended time of petition and praise!

Can we say a word here about asking people to volunteer their time? We know that most members of a Christian organization will have a strong desire to undergird that organization in prayer at all times. However, if times of corporate prayer are relegated to "after-hours," the message we transmit is: "The work is more important than prayer. Consequently, we haven't time to stop working to pray. We'll have to do that after we're through working." You get the point . . . . Earlier, we noted the weekly investment World Vision makes as we call together four hundred of our staff members for an hour of time together.

Prayer Retreats

At World Vision we have made it a practice to have each working unit, whether it be a division or a department, take a day as a group away from the office. Many times this can be used for praying about specific needs of the work unit. Again, the message given is that people are important as individuals and their spiritual contribution is a vital part of the organization.

Spontaneity in Prayer

This is where your individual leadership is really needed. Others are not going to feel comfortable with breaking into a discussion or a meeting with a suggestion that this might be an appropriate time for prayer unless you take the lead in doing it.

How easy it is to be driven by the urgency of the matter, the schedule of the next meeting, or the pressure of the next appointment to believe that we probably don't have time to pray.

A Ministry of Prayer

People who are given a special ministry of prayer need to be encouraged and undergirded. The local church needs a band of individuals with whom to share special prayer requests.

For the Christian organization, this may mean building up a group of people who will commit themselves to support that organization in prayer. For example, World Vision International has a ministry which we call International Intercessors. Over ten thousand individuals have agreed to receive monthly information about how they can offer their prayers of petition or praise in support of our work.

"Now May the God of Peace . . .

. . . who brought again from the dead our Lord Jesus, the great shepherd of the sheep, by the blood of the eternal covenant, equip you with everything good that you may do his will, working in you that which is pleasing in his sight, through Jesus Christ; to whom be glory forever and ever. Amen" (Heb. 13: 20, 21).

Part IV

The Language of Management

Glossary

Every art or science has its own language or jargon. Here is a dictionary of terms you may find useful:

ABC's: A technique for ranking ideas or items by first assigning them into categories—A equals *very important,* high value; B equals *somewhat important,* medium value; C equals *less important,* low value. The same technique may then be used to further subdivide each of the categories constructed.

Accounting: The system of recording and summarizing business and financial transactions and analyzing, verifying, and reporting results. You need it.

Account Number: A specific number assigned for a category of expenditures, assets or liabilities.

Activity: Work carried out under a specific cost center.

Activity Report: A report written, usually to a superior, outlining the work done during the previous reporting period.

Administration: A body of persons in charge (they administer!).

Assets: Items on the balance sheet showing book value of property owned.

Assumption: The view of reality held by the individual or individuals when making decisions or plans. Too often assumptions are left unstated, with disastrous results.

Authority: 1) The right to make a decision within a specific area of responsibility, such as the authority to hire or fire. 2) The person holding this right, as in the expression "a higher authority."

Balance Sheet: A statement of a financial condition at a given date.

Bar Chart: A diagram used to show events and schedule of an overall plan. The length of the bars, which usually run horizontally, relate to time. Sometimes called a *Gantt Chart.*

Board of Advisors: Usually a group of specialists or authorities in a field who are willing to lend their name and their technical expertise to an organization.

Board of Directors: The governing body of an organization.

Board of Reference: Individuals who have been willing to lend their name and reputation to an organization. A Board of Reference usually has no authority or administrative control.

Bookkeeping: Recording of accounts or transactions. *Not* accounting.

Budget: Financial plans which tell how an organization or office expects to spend funds over a given period of time.

CEO: Abbreviation for Chief Executive Officer.

CPM: Abbreviation for Critical Path Method, a planning tool similar to PERT.

Calling: Generally one's vocation. Used by most Christians to describe the work for which they believe God has prepared them.

Change: The transformation of a normal procedure, series of events, or other way of going about the organization's business to a new situation, procedure or routine.

Change Agent: A role played by those who are attempting to help an organization bring about planned change.

Chart of Accounts: A listing and definition of categories of expenditures, assets or liabilities. Gives the accountant the names and numbers for each account.

Chief Executive Officer: Title given to cover a wide range of other titles, such as executive director, president, chairman of the board, given to an individual who has ultimate responsibility for the *operation* of an organization.

Christian Priorities: As used by the authors, the idea that there are three levels of priorities for the Christian and the Christian organization: 1) Commitment to God and Christ; 2) commitment to the body of Christ, his church; and 3) commitment to the work of Christ.

Conflict: The normal difference of opinion that arises as individuals seek to plan for or to achieve goals. Conflicts should be viewed as healthy.

Cost Center: A budgeting and accounting term used to indicate one or more related activities.

Delegation: The act of assigning to another person specific acts or responsibilities for which the delegator is normally responsible.

Direct Cost: Cost that can be directly related to a project or cost center. When an accountant sees an invoice for a purchased item and can specifically identify that item with a particular project, the amount on the invoice is the direct cost.

Discretionary Time: The time during working hours under the direct control of the individual, as opposed to superior imposed time or peer imposed time.

Employee Review: A regular evaluation by the organization's management to measure the employee's performance against the job description.

Enabler: A person who by his or her actions enhances the ablity of others to carry out their desired task.

Entry: The accounting term to describe a notation in a ledger or journal.

Evaluation: The act of reviewing previous events or actions to see whether they conform with expected results. Most organizations could use a lot more of this!

Event: A planning term used to describe a completed action. Sometimes used interchangeably with milestone.

Executive: A general title given to a person of responsibility within the organization who is not involved in the direct supervision of the day-to-day work of others. A knowledge worker.

Executive Committee: Usually a subcommittee of the board of directors which acts in an executive capacity when the board is not in session.

Exempt employee: An employee, usually a manager or executive, whose job exempts him from being subject to overtime payment through the U.S. Fair Labor Act.

Expectations: Description of outcomes, goals or future events.

Facilitator: An individual whose task is to assist the organization or group through some process, usually a meeting, seminar or group dynamics.

Facility: Something designed, built, installed, and so on, to serve a specific function, for example a building.

Firefighting: Responding to the emergencies of the moment as opposed to concentrating on the longer, sometimes less exciting, work that leads to a successful future.

Goal: A desired result which lies in the future. As we use the term, we define it as a measurable (in time and space), an accomplishable future event. Some people use "goal" interchangeably with "objective." Other people use such terms as senior goal, intermediate goal, line goal, and other terminology to indicate that some goals are dependent upon others.

Gantt Chart: A bar chart that uses hollow bars which are filled up to indicate elapsed time. See *Bar Chart.*

General ledger: A system of accounts classifying transactions to summarize their total amounts for a specific period of time.

Group process: Usually used to describe the working together of a group in an open and supporting way such that decisions or actions agreed upon are viewed by the members of the group as being owned by all members of the group.

In-house: Activities or work carried out within the organization by the employees of the organization.

Input: Energy, resources, and knowledge which is applied to produce a desired output or result.

Insider: A member of the organization.

Job description: A description of the authority, responsibility, actions, and qualifications of a position. Not a description of work of a particular individual. Rather a description of what that individual is supposed to be doing. Sometimes called a position description.

Journal: An accounting term for a book in which records are kept.

Knowledge worker: A person primarily involved in work which requires knowledge and mental skills as opposed to technical or physical skills.

Leader: A person who has followers in a given situation.

Levels of delegation: The extent to which responsibility to act or to sign has been delegated.

Line: Those members of the organization who have a direct responsibility for the desired outcomes and goals of the organization. Used as opposed to *Staff.*

Lines of Authority: A description of the sequence of relationships between individuals and the organization which have to do with an individual's authority to make decisions or to give orders. In the military it is known as chain-of-command.

Lines of Communication: A description of the relationship between individuals and the organization that indicates the way information is to be transmitted through the organization.

Long-range planning: Planning which attempts to anticipate the distant future. The length of time will vary between the different types of organizations. More than three years is usually considered long-range planning.

Lose/lose: The results of an action in which both parties involved do not benefit from the outcome. See *Win/win* and *Win/lose.*

MBO: Management by objective.

Manager: An executive responsible for the outcome of a program or project.

Management by objective: A style of management which focuses its energies on desired predetermined objectives by relating the objectives of each suborganization within the organization and each individual within the organization to the total objectives of the organization.

Management by results: Similar to management by objectives except generally considered to go a step further and anticipate the overall results that will occur as a result of meeting objectives.

Man-hour: An hour of work by one person, used as a measured amount of time to do a job. For example, five man-hours is five persons working for one hour or one person working for five hours. Some organizations are using the term "person-hour."

Manpower: The number of persons available or required to accomplish some task. For example, the manpower needed for this job is five people for two weeks. Also called "people-power."

Means: Anything involved in converting plans into actions.

Methods: Specific ways of carrying out a task or solving a problem.

Milestone: The end result of an activity which results in an event. Sometimes called a subgoal.

Norm: The way things are usually done or outcomes that are usually expected. Not necessarily a specified procedure, but generally understood by the group or organization. Norms have to do with such things as mode of dress, customs of greeting, orientation, and so on.

Objective: A desired end result, usually measurable in time and performance. See *Goal.*

Organizing: The act of bringing together the individuals and resources within an organization to obtain the desired objective of the organization.

Organization chart: A diagram showing the relationships, usually of authority, between different members of the organization.

Organizational life style: A general description of the way the organization conducts itself, a picture of its own self-understanding, those things which differentiate it from other organizations.

Orientation: The process of introducing a new staff member into the norms, procedures, and policies of the organization.

Outsider: Someone who is not a member of the organization.

Out-of-house: Work done outside of the organization by those who are not members of the organization.

Overhead: An accounting term referring to costs which cannot be specified as direct costs and therefore must be taken into account in the total operation of the organization. Some Christian organizations use this term to mean everything not connected with their direct ministry. See *Process.*

PERT: An acronym standing for *Program Evaluation Review Technique.* A logic diagram which shows the relationship between events needed to accomplish a goal. The relationship is shown by lines of dependency which represent the amount of time needed to accomplish each event. PERT and the Critical Path Method (CPM) are similar to one another in that the two terms are sometimes used interchangeably.

PR: Public Relations. Euphemism used to cover the activities of an organization in an attempt to describe its actions to its constituency.

People-power: The name of individuals available to accomplish a task within an organization. A word used in an attempt to demasculinize "manpower."

Plan: A detailed description of events necessary to reach a goal. This may be displayed a number of ways, such as on a PERT chart, a Gantt chart, a bar chart, or just a list of items. A complete plan should not only show the events but the time and resources needed to accomplish each event and, thus, the total time and resources needed to reach the goal.

Planning: The process of discovering the optimum way to reach a goal and a description of the necessary events, resources, and time needed to reach it.

Policy: A statement or statements which attempt to establish the boundaries or framework within which the organization will carry out its procedures. Policies are usually established by the governing body of the organization.

Position description: See *Job description.*

Post: To make an entry in an accounting journal.

Practice: Normal method by which an organization goes about reaching a specific goal.

Procedure: The detailed steps necessary to reach a goal. Procedure usually implies that there is a normal way of going about the task.

Progress report: A regular report, weekly, biweekly, or perhaps monthly, made to higher authority describing progress toward goals during a previous reporting period.

Purpose: An aim, the general reason for which the organization exists. Goals support a purpose.

Reporting time: The elapsed time between progress reports and/or the time covered by a progress report.

Resources: Money, property, and/or people necessary or available to reach a goal. Resources are a form of input.

Scenario: A description of the possible course of future events. Scenarios are used as a version of planning to attempt to write "future history." The usual procedure is then to write an "optimistic scenario" and a "pessimistic scenario" in an attempt to anticipate as many contingencies as possible.

Seminar: A short learning experience, usually with active participation by the learners.

Short range plan: A plan which covers only a short period of time, usually less than one year. See *Long-range planning.*

Span of control: The number of individuals reporting to one person.

The larger the number of individuals, the wider is the span of control.

Staff: Members of the organization not directly responsible for the goals of the organization. Staff members usually report to "line" positions.

Staffing: The act of recruiting, engaging, and orienting individuals to previously defined positions within the organization. See *Job description.*

Standard: A description of a desired result against which performance can be measured. Some organizations use the term instead of subgoal.

Standard day: An ideal schedule for an executive's day. The idea of a standard day is to allot certain portions of each day to certain tasks so that both the executive, and those who relate to him or her, can anticipate what time will be available for a certain class of tasks. A standard day is almost always an ideal and is used as a point of departure rather than a hard and fast rule.

Standard week: Similar to a standard day, only with variations between days.

Status quo: Another term for the rut we are in.

Subgoal: A goal which supports another goal and is needed to accomplish the higher goal.

Supervisor: A person responsible for detail performance of other employees on a day-to-day basis.

Things-to-do list: An informal list prepared by an individual of items of work to be accomplished during the near future. An informal personal plan.

Verbal fog: Cloud of words used to hide real meaning.

Work log: A diary kept by an employee to describe the type of work done during specific hours and the amount of time for each item. Often used by individuals who are paid directly by the hour, such as a lawyer, or by those who want to improve the effectiveness of their own time estimating.

Work schedule: A detailed plan for carrying out a series of events to reach a goal which shows time needed for each event and time and/or date when it will be completed.

Win/Lose: An outcome in which one individual loses and the other one wins.

Win/Win: An outcome in which both parties are advantaged by the resulting circumstances. The most desirable result. See *Lose/lose.*

Bibliography

Alinsky, Saul D., *Rules for Radicals.* New York: Random House, Inc., 1972.

Becker, Ernest. *The Denial of Death.* New York: Free Press, 1973.

Bolles, Richard Nelson. *What Color Is Your Parachute?* Berkeley, Calif.: Ten Speed Press, 1972.

Booth, Catherine. *Female Ministry.* Los Angeles: Salvation Army, 1859.

Cavalier, Richard. *Achieving Objectives in Meetings.* New York: Program Counsel, 1973.

Crosby, Philip B. *The Art of Getting Your Own Sweet Way.* New York: McGraw-Hill Book Company, 1972.

Dale, Ernest. *Organization.* New York: American Management Association, 1967.

Dayton, Edward R. *God's Purpose/Man's Plans.* Monrovia, Calif.: MARC, 1974.

————. *Tools for Time Management.* Grand Rapids: Zondervan Publishing House, 1974.

———— and Engstrom, Ted W. *Strategy for Living.* Glendale, Calif.: Regal Books, 1976.

————. *Strategy for Leadership.* Old Tappan: Revell, 1979.

Drucker, Peter. *Age of Discontinuity.* New York: Harper & Row, 1969.

————. *The Effective Executive.* New York: Harper & Row, 1967.

Engstrom, Ted W. *The Making of a Christian Leader.* Grand Rapids: Zondervan Publishing House, 1976.

———— and Dayton, Edward R. *The Art of Management for Christian Leaders.* Waco: Word Books, Publisher, 1976.

Ewing, David W. *The Human Side of Planning.* New York: Macmillan & Co., 1969.

————. *Writing for Results.* New York: John Wiley & Sons, 1974.

Gangel, Kenneth. *So You Want to Be a Leader.* Harrisburg: Christian Publications, Inc., 1973.

Gross, Malvern J. *Financial and Accounting Guide for Non-Profit Organizations.* New York: Ronald Press, 1974.

Johnson, David W. and Johnson, Frank P. *Joining Together: Group Theory and Group Skills.* Englewood Cliffs: Prentice-Hall, 1975.

Johnson, James L. *The Nine-to-Five Complex, or the Christian Organization Man.* Grand Rapids: Zondervan Publishing House, 1972.

Korn, S. Winton and Boyd, Thomas. *Managerial Accounting.* New York: John Wiley & Sons, Inc., 1975.

Kotler, Philip. *Marketing for Non-Profit Organizations*. Englewood Cliffs: Prentice-Hall, 1975.

Larson, Roland S. and Larson, Doris E. *Values and Faith*. Minneapolis: Winston Press, 1976.

Likert, Rensis and Likert, Jane Gibson. *New Ways of Managing Conflict*. New York: McGraw-Hill Book Company, 1976.

Linden, Eugene. *The Alms Race*. New York: Random House, 1976.

Luft, Joseph. *Group Processes: An Introduction to Group Dynamics*. Palo Alto, Calif.: Mayfield Publishing Co., 1970.

Mackenzie, Alec. *The Time Trap: Managing Your Way Out*. New York: American Management Association, 1972.

Mager, Robert. *Goal Analysis*. Belmont, Calif.: Fearon, 1972.

May, Rollo. *The Courage to Create*. New York: W. W. Norton & Company, Inc., 1975.

Ortlund, Raymond and Ortlund, Anne. *The Second Half of Life*. Glendale, Calif.: Regal Books, 1976.

Sanders, J. Oswald. *Spiritual Leadership*. Chicago: Moody Press, 1974.

Schaller, Lyle E. *The Change Agent*. Nashville: Abingdon Press, 1972.

———. *Parish Planning*. Nashville: Abingdon Press, 1971.

Sheehy, Gail. *Passages*. New York: E. P. Dutton & Company, Inc., 1976.

Sheff, Alexander L. *Bookkeeping Made Easy*. New York: Barnes & Noble, 1971.

Tournier, Paul. *Learn to Grow Old*. New York: Harper & Row, Publishers, 1973.

Williams, Don. *The Apostle Paul and Women in the Church*. Van Nuys, Calif.: BIM Publishing Co., 1977.

Index